FriesenPress

One Printers Way
Altona, MB R0G 0B0
Canada

www.friesenpress.com

Copyright © 2022 by Al Galloway
First Edition — 2022

ISBN
978-1-03-913387-7 (Hardcover)
978-1-03-913386-0 (Paperback)
978-1-03-913388-4 (eBook)

1. Biography & Autobiography, Sports

Distributed to the trade by The Ingram Book Company

TABLE OF CONTENTS

DEDICATION

For my parents, Jack and Helen Galloway, my wife
Doreen, son Jason and my brother Bob. Their love and
support mean more to me than they will ever know.

FOREWORD

By Chris Cuthbert

It's safe to say that Foster Hewitt had an enormous impact on my life, even if I was never fortunate enough to meet the iconic voice of Hockey Night in Canada.

Throughout my childhood I would be serenaded to sleep at night by Foster's call of Leaf games, emanating from his hallowed Gondola perch at Maple Leaf Gardens in Toronto or from other Original Six outposts from Boston to Chicago on CKFH or CBC Radio.

I didn't realize that at the time I was subconsciously studying the nuances of Hewitt's call, the inflection which would command a listener's attention, a soundtrack that created an anticipation that something special was about to happen.

But in my youth, I was equally captivated by the background stories of athletes, their roots, career paths, and, in many cases, the obstacles which they overcame to achieve greatness.

During my elementary school years, I read countless sports books to garner a greater appreciation for what set championship athletes apart. In this vein, it wasn't Foster Hewitt who provided inspiration, but his father W.A. Hewitt, who authored a book of Great Canadian Sports Heroes.

By the age of 12 I had probably reread the book a half dozen times, mesmerized by the standout achievements of early Canadian champions and their paths to glory.

Part of my fascination might have been because then, unlike today, the stories of Canadian sport greatness beyond hockey were limited. I can't imagine that there were lengthy, multi layered debates among Lou Marsh Trophy voters in the 50's and 60's as there might have been in the recent years of Canada's tsunami of success in a variety of amateur and professional sports. In 2021 alone, Olympic decathlon champion Damian Warner won the award as Canada's best athlete, outpolling many worthy contenders including sprinter Andre De Grasse, hockey superstar Conner McDavid, tennis phenom Leylah Annie Fernandez, soccer stars Stephanie Labbe' and Alphonso Davies and swimmer Maggie MacNeil.

But there is a common thread among successful athletes in lean and bumper crop years. On the path to greatness there are often daunting obstacles to conquer. In W.A. Hewitt's book, it was those athletes who overcame what appeared to be insurmountable odds to reach the pinnacle who left a lasting imprint.

Over a half century later, I can still recall the story of Douglas Hepburn, born with a club foot and cross eyed, who suffered the verbal slings of schoolmates, but found a way to succeed by discovering his raison d'etre in the weight room to transform himself into the world's strongest man.

I've had a lifelong fascination with the story of Tom Longboat, who endured and later escaped residential school, running away from discrimination and world class marathon fields to win the Boston Marathon and World Professional championship, to be recognized as the premier distance runner of his time.

Percy Williams, Canada's first Olympic hero, the 100 and 200 metre gold medalist in Amsterdam, was diagnosed with rheumatic fever in childhood. Doctors cautioned his parents from allowing Percy to engage in any strenuous activity which could potentially damage his heart. But Williams' heart was stronger than anyone could have imagined.

Almost a century later the inspirational stories of athletes' triumphs over adversity are many; Michael Phelps overcoming ADHD to become the most decorated Olympian. Hockey's cancer survivors, Mario Lemieux, Brian Boyle, and Oskar Lindblom to name just a few.

Naomi Osaka, Mardy Fish and Simone Biles have opened the dialogue on mental health issues among high performance athletes. As our world becomes increasingly complex, the obstacles potentially facing all of us have increased exponentially. Racial discrimination, sexual and gender orientation issues, the widening socioeconomic gap, HIV, CTE, the list seems endless.

What remains timeless is the ability of so many to endure, overcome and inspire. In that regard, Al Galloway's collection of stories from ordinary Canadians doing extraordinary things is a "chicken soup" offering of comfort, hope and motivation.

I've known Al since we were teens and although I was aware of his affliction, I only saw a friend who persevered, with a self-deprecating sense of humour, without self-pity or complaint, even if an unsteady hand forced him to miss his share of short putts. No matter how close our friendship I couldn't truly understand the extent of his trials without walking in his shoes. Galloway's collection of stories sheds light on the plight of others who have faced adversity and illuminates the glory of their triumphs.

I can't begin to compare my story with any which Al has chronicled, but I can relate to the barriers which each of us face and must confront to achieve our most cherished goals and dreams.

In those formative years listening to Foster Hewitt, I envisioned being that voice on the radio, a soundtrack of hockey, in some small way like the iconic Hockey Night in Canada voice. My personal barricade was a fear of public speaking, a fear which I have yet to fully conquer. There have been panic attacks and missed and rejected opportunities resulting from my insecurity and personal kryptonite.

While attending Queen's University I realized that I needed to confront that fear if I was ever, realistically, going to chase my ultimate life goal. Eventually, I enrolled in a Public Speaking Anxiety course conducted by the Psychology faculty. On the first day I nervously paced by the open class numerous times before finally summoning the courage to walk through the door. It was one small, but essential step on my way to the Hockey Night in Canada broadcast booth.

Al Galloway's book, Inspired, Healing Journeys from Hockey and Beyond chronicles a collection of remarkable individuals who have taken far more courageous steps, to confront significantly greater life challenges, to turn, in some cases, tragedy into triumph.

Take the next step, turn the page, and be Inspired by this collection of stories of common folks and their uncommonly extraordinary and motivational lives.

CHAPTER ONE

My Story

"If you are always trying to be normal, you will never know how amazing you can be."

MAYA ANGELOU
American poet, singer, memoirist,
and civil rights activist

W here to begin. Like so many boomers born in the mid-1950s, there is so much history to consider. Mass media has dominated our lives. Man walked on the moon. Diseases like polio were all but eliminated. Paul Henderson single-handedly showed those dastardly Soviets who the greatest hockey nation on the planet was. And mankind was on a continual march to make my generation the luckiest and most successful ever.

I was born into all of this in January 1956 to a father who worked as a white-collar employee of the Ford Motor Company and a stay-at-home mother. Seven years younger than my brother, my parents had wondered if they would ever have another child. Their journey and mine had begun.

We lived at 1764 Kildare Road in Windsor, Ontario, in a small two-bedroom bungalow. At first, nothing seemed out of the ordinary. I was somewhat small, but otherwise active and healthy. Other than not being overly gifted at math, music, and swimming, I enjoyed reasonable success at most things.

Jack and Helen Galloway, like virtually all parents of the time, wanted a life for my brother Bob and me that was better than their generation enjoyed.

They were products of the Great Depression, World War II, and the Cold War. They were of modest financial means and believed that hard work and knowing your station in life were the keys to success.

When I was eight, my father's job was transferred to the Town of Brampton, Ontario, near Toronto. We settled into our new home at 217 Mill Street South. At the time, Brampton was a small community of around twenty thousand people, and the move marked a decidedly different existence than the one I had known in industrial Windsor.

I was a somewhat shy child, and as such, I struggled to settle into my new life and new school, and to make new friends. To compound this, during the final two years of my life in Windsor, I had begun exhibiting signs of issues that, in years to come, would come to define my life and career path.

These issues consisted of repeated throat clearing, excessive blinking and sporadic shrugging of my head and shoulders. For the most part my parents, on the advice of the family doctor, hoped that I was simply an anxious, if not extra nervous, child and that I would eventually outgrow these symptoms.

As winter settled in after our move to Brampton, my parents registered me in hockey. I would never evolve beyond house league. I was a decent skater. I even managed as a left winger, to get a reasonable number of breakaways. But as one early coach put it, my shot could not break a pane of glass. Thus, my path to the NHL was thwarted.

As I grew during elementary school, I became increasingly interested in sports. My classmates, hockey teammates, and I were fans of the National Hockey League (NHL) (the Toronto Maple Leafs mostly), the Canadian Football League, and Major League Baseball. Pick-up games of shinny on local ponds, road hockey on our quiet streets, and baseball and football in the school yard made up most of our existence outside of school. And if we were not playing sports, we were watching them on TV or listening to them on radio. The men who broadcast these games (women were not yet part of sports broadcasts) would become as important to my friends and me as the athletes themselves. I would find myself calling hockey, play by play, as I watched Hockey Night in Canada with the volume turned off. At the same time, I was dreaming about what it would be like to be Bill Hewitt or Danny Gallivan calling the action.

Meanwhile, the physical issues I began exhibiting in Windsor at age six, were not going away. In fact, they were becoming increasingly frequent and more noticeable. And while my parents loved me, they were at a loss to understand or explain them. For them, they were not only inexplicable, but also somewhat embarrassing, both for them and me. I was becoming more and more uncomfortable around kids my age. I would come home upset, as I felt that everyone was watching and judging me for not being able to stop or even control my motions.

Thus, came more trips to the family doctor. Again, he expressed the thought that I was simply a very anxious person. But, at the request of my parents, he referred me to a child psychiatrist, and ultimately, I was prescribed sedatives. Little orange pills that not only made me feel lethargic, but also a failure. Why couldn't I just be normal, like all the other kids?

By the time I had moved on to high school, the pills were discontinued. With them, I still displayed the same issues, only as a more sluggish, subdued version of myself. I was increasingly less confident around my peers and looked for every excuse I could to hang out with the adults in my life. Around them, I was a virtual chatterbox, while around my friends, I was introverted and insecure.

Self-confidence became increasingly difficult for me to come by through high school. Grade nine was a huge challenge for me, as I was sometimes bullied by one classmate. My parents saw me coming home upset but felt powerless to help. In desperation, they turned once again to our family doctor to talk with me. But, when he broached the subject with me, I withdrew into myself and would not discuss it with him. It embarrassed me, and it was easier to simply pretend nothing was wrong.

I got through the high school years with a small, but closely knit, group of friends and tried not to draw attention to myself. I had to try to blend in. To appear normal. To stand out only invited inevitable taunting and teasing. Even when I was part of a team that won a provincial schoolboy curling championship in Grade Twelve, I was uncomfortable with the attention.

Don't be a failure. But don't be overly successful either. These would only bring attention to my issues. Thus, I was an average student. And I was just good enough in school to be admitted to McMaster University (Mac) in Hamilton, Ontario, about an hour's drive west of Toronto. As a History Major, I thought maybe I would become a teacher. My time there was pretty much non-descript, and for the first three years, uneventful.

It was at Mac that my lifelong interest in broadcasting would take an interesting turn. In year three, our campus radio station was granted an FM license. When I began my fourth year, I resolved to overcome my fear of being noticed and join the station's sports department. Mostly, I prepared and read weekend sports updates. But I also got some experience covering live hockey, basketball, and football games. I even read the news on occasion. I was hooked. When I interviewed the hockey, basketball and football players, I was so nervous that I was shaking like leaf. I was undeterred, however.

Broadcasting was challenging. Part of me wanted to standout and part of me wanted not to be noticed. Thanks to my mother's encouragement, I was always a surprisingly good public speaker. In fact, at eight years of age, CHIC Radio in Brampton was doing a live remote broadcast in a men's clothing store while my parents were shopping for clothes with my brother. I was fascinated watching the DJ. He noticed me standing there and invited me to join him on air for an interview. I still remember my father's face as he heard me on air and turned to see me with the DJ.

From that day, I loved broadcasting and thought of performing on TV or Radio. I desperately wanted to overcome my reservations and chase my radio and TV dream. Unsure how to proceed, during my final year at Mac, I made an unsolicited visit to CFNY-FM radio in my hometown. The Program Director, for some reason, decided to come out and talk to me. Since I was about to graduate from Mac, he suggested I do a feature report on McMaster's famous Medical School Program. If it was deemed worthy, they would air it on the station.

So, I reached out to the Dean of the Med School and was granted an interview. We spoke in his office several days later for over an hour. I returned to the studios of the campus radio station to edit the story. To my horror I discovered not one word of the interview made it to tape. What now? Do I ask for a second interview? Or do I take the high road and explain my egregious action to the Program Director at CFNY and hope for the best? Instead, I did what every aspiring young broadcaster would do—I decided that what every honourable radio guy would do was to walk away from the circumstance, and not contact the station at all, and never speak of it again (until now).

Thus, my big chance was gone. What next? After some soul searching, I decided to cast my net by placing an ad in RPM Magazine offering my services as a sportscaster. I was identified only by an anonymous box number at the magazine. Lo and behold, I received a response looking for someone to join a Yorkton Saskatchewan radio station that was looking for someone to do play by play of the Junior A Yorkton Terriers hockey club, in addition to morning and afternoon sports updates.

It sounded perfect, except for my lack of self-confidence. So, when push came to shove, following graduation from Mac, I passed on the opportunity and did not even respond to the Yorkton station. The good news is that it did not go to waste as I brought it to a friend's attention, and he has gone on to a successful broadcasting career of his own. At the time, I was not consciously aware of the role that my inexplicable physical behaviours had in this decision. There is no doubt in my mind now, though, that it played a huge part in it.

Instead, I attended an interview arranged by my father for a "safe" career in the automotive industry. It was with the Ford Motor Company in Oakville, Ontario. I was hired by Ford, despite feeling unqualified for the job and very insecure about how receptive the automotive world would be to my "quirks." The job involved manually preparing and delivering parts sales reports to various executives at Head Office. I had no business training or experience, and I felt like a fraud. I worried incessantly that I would be discovered by those I worked with, that they would find out that I was very much in over my head.

Thus began a thirty-seven-year career in the automotive industry that would bring about its share of frustration. It was made clear when I was hired that working there would involve considerable moving around the country, often with little or no notice. Sure enough, just eight months into my life at Ford, I was transferred to Edmonton. I was told by my boss in Oakville that they were eliminating my role at head office. I could accept a lay-off or fly the next day to Edmonton for an interview at the Regional Office there. Following a whirlwind trip and interview, I was expected to give my bosses at Ford an immediate decision to accept or decline the position. I felt I had no choice but to accept the move.

Edmonton would bring about new challenges. For the first time in my life, I was without the safety net of family and friends. I knew nobody there. I felt truly alone, doing a job I was unprepared for. I arrived in early April 1980, just as Pierre Trudeau was embroiled with the province of Alberta over Energy Policy. People there were not very receptive when they found out I was from big bad Ontario. I had a lot of time on my hands to think. I decided I was not happy with my current lot in life. Should I resign from Ford and return to Ontario? Not just yet!

For the second time in my life, I reached out through RPM Magazine. I placed another anonymous classified ad looking for potential sportscasting opportunities. Once again, I got a response. And, as fate would have it, this chance to do something I loved was in Alberta. It was located a five-hour drive north of Edmonton, in Grande Prairie.

I spent a weekend in Peace River country for an interview with the Program Director at an a.m. station. We spoke for over an hour as he proudly explained to me how they were on the "cutting edge" of Canadian broadcasting history by becoming the second AM station in the nation to broadcast in stereo. Look out FM.

He had me do a demo in studio where I nervously read a sportscast. When I finished, he suggested that I was not quite the "right fit," but he offered to call the other station in town so that I could go speak with them.

As I left that interview, I walked out totally deflated. I decided, as I ate lunch, not to pursue the other opportunity. I did not even show up at the other station to discuss it. Maybe I was not meant to be a broadcaster after all. I returned to Edmonton to continue at Ford, while I pondered my future. By October, I had decided to return home to Ontario. I handed in my resignation and prepared to drive home on Halloween, 1980, just six months after arriving in Alberta. I had no idea what my working future would hold. The answer would present itself two days before I was to leave Edmonton. I was asked to interview for a position in a new department at Ford in Oakville that would be known as the Vehicle Order Centre. I would be assisting dealers with their vehicle ordering issues.

Looking back, several red flags were presented to me during my interview upon my return to Oakville. It was made clear to me that most management types would not look fondly at me returning from "the opportunity of a lifetime." In fact, the interviewer suggested people would think I must have "two heads" for even daring to turn my back on Edmonton. I felt, however, as if I had to take the job in Oakville, if even just to repay the bank loan I had taken when I bought a new Mercury Capri just prior to finding out about the transfer to Edmonton.

My interviewer was right. Management made it clear to me for the next eight and half years that opportunities to advance at Ford would be hard to come by. I was forever judged for my "transgressions." I hung in there until June of 1989. I felt trapped, with no other way to earn a living. It was then that an acquaintance I had worked with, Bruce Craigie, had moved on to work for Honda and Acura. He helped me secure a job as a District Sales Manager there. I grew and in my own shy way, enjoyed some limited success. It was there that Bruce, through my wife Doreen, eventually convinced me to get some help with my "quirks." They were being noticed by management, and they were not helping my career prospects.

This meant yet another visit to the family physician. It took some effort to convince him that I could no longer ignore the "elephant in the room," but he referred me to the Motion Disorder Clinic at Toronto's Western Hospital, and I finally got a diagnosis. I had Tourette's Syndrome (TS).

As defined on the Tourette Canada Web Site…

"Tourette's Syndrome (TS) is a Neurodevelopmental or brain-based condition that causes people who have it to make involuntary sounds and movements called tics." Tics are defined by Tourette Canada as "sudden, intermittent, repetitive, unpredictable, purposeless, nonrhythmic, involuntary movements or sounds. Tics that produce movement are called motor tics, while those that produce sounds are called vocal tics or phonic tics."

It seems that following nearly thirty years of feeling like I should be able to control my actions, I would now have to adjust to a new reality—I would have to come to accept that these were not my fault, even if others might still not understand or accept them.

Now that I could define why I did what I did, the next question was what to do about it? And at the behest of Doreen, I consulted with one more psychiatrist, who prescribed a low dose of a drug known as Pimozide. The scary part was that it is used in the treatment of psychotic conditions, which, as far as I know, do not include me. But after some reassurance, I began taking it and continue to do so to this day.

While the control of my tics is not total, the drug has provided me with excellent results. One thing I have noticed, over thirty-plus years taking my medication, is that I have developed a tremor in my hands. The medical profession cannot tell me definitively that this is caused by the drug. It is, however, listed as a possible side-effect. Unlike with Parkinson's, I do not have this tremor when my hands are at rest, and it is more predominant in my right hand than my left. It seems to present itself when I move my hands in certain ways. Cursive writing anything other than signing my name (albeit illegibly) is virtually impossible. Using eating utensils or a screwdriver can be practically hilarious at times. Forget about shaving! And fans of my TV career have probably noticed a shaky microphone when I am conducting interviews.

To this point, I had spent my life dealing with feelings of inadequacy and powerlessness. Until my TS diagnosis, I had spent my life trying to be in full control of all situations. I had tried many things to achieve control in my life. Prior to the Tourette's diagnosis, I had turned to medication, counselling, and self-help such as Dale Carnegie Training. I even went to weekly sessions with a registered "Hypnotherapist" for a while. Nothing though, provided me with the confidence and the degree of control over my tics the Pimozide would bring.

As my twenties turned into my thirties, my confidence was slowly growing, even prior to my diagnosis. By my late twenties, I worked up the courage to "put myself out there more." Once again, enter my colleague and friend, Bruce Craigie. While we were both working together at Ford, he had told me about being part of Big Brothers as a mentor to a child without a father figure in his life. I was thinking about finding ways I, too, could "give back." I was not involved in a serious relationship at the time, and felt I had time I could offer as a Big Brother. And thus began the first of the two most significant relationships in my life to this day.

Ten-year-old Jason and I became a team, and as our relationship developed, I became close to his whole extended family. By extension, that meant his mother and I developed a relationship as well. After I turned thirty-four, Doreen and I were married. Tourette's meant that I was always reluctant to become seriously involved with most relationships because that would mean relinquishing control. It would mean revealing my deepest, darkest fears and my lack of self-confidence. Jason and Doreen have played a huge role in helping me learn to deal with this. At the time of writing, Doreen and I have been happily married for thirty years, and still going strong. There have been good times and tough times, and hopefully, there will be many more of both. But, as with all relationships, these are still very much a work in progress, and I would not trade them for anything.

As my self-belief increased, I came more and more to the realization that something was still missing in my life. That was the world of broadcasting. More specifically, sportscasting. And in the late summer of 1988, I picked up the telephone and contacted my local cable tv provider (Cablenet). I was put in touch with the Sports Producer, Brad Scott. I would scratch my broadcasting itch as a volunteer covering Junior Hockey, curling, golf, baseball, football, and lacrosse. I would also add public service, political debates, parades, and other programming to my resume. That was the one "broadcasting interview" I did not walk away from.

Over the years, Cablenet morphed into Cogeco TV, and later, Your TV. I also provided coverage of Ontario Curling Championships and Ontario Hockey League action on both Rogers TV and Your TV. And as the years have gone by, I have enjoyed a wealth of experiences, and made many longstanding friendships. Self-belief is an on-going struggle, but I have grown exponentially thanks to this time on television across Ontario.

By now, I hope it has become apparent, that I am something of a late bloomer. Our lives are, in many ways, products of our experiences and the resulting decisions we've made, and, when strung together over the years, they offer challenges we must all overcome. While at this stage of life, I am not likely to ever announce NHL Hockey or become President of an automotive company, I am proud that I have persisted with overcoming my challenges and finally become happy with how my life has evolved. Everyone in my life, including Doreen and Jason, my parents, my brother Bob, and all my friends and colleagues share in whatever successes I have achieved.

Which brings me to this book. After all these years, I have come to realize that everyone has struggles and challenges to overcome in life. The decisions we make as we face these challenges define us, for better or worse. The chapters that follow tell the stories of people, who like me, have had circumstances to overcome in life, things they did not allow to define them for the worse; people who have faced adversity and gone on to achieve great things. I hope their stories will serve to entertain, inform, and inspire you as you deal with what life has to offer. I know they have inspired me.

CHAPTER TWO
Ed Burkholder

---

*"I've never known a man worth his salt who in the long
run, deep down in his heart, didn't appreciate the grind, the
discipline...I firmly believe that any man's finest hour—this
greatest fulfillment to all he holds dear—is the moment
when he has worked his heart out in a good cause and lies
exhausted on the field of battle—victorious."*

VINCE LOMBARDI
National Football League Coach

Look out world, Ed Burkholder had arrived. I am not certain Murray and Helen Burkholder realized the impact their sixth child would have when he was born in Stratford, Ontario in February 1968. But, looking back, I am certain that impact has been profound.

Murray was a Manager with London Life Insurance. Helen was a Nurse with a master's degree. By the time Ed was two years of age, the family had moved back to the Niagara Region. First, in Niagara Falls, and shortly thereafter, to 32 Glen View in Welland. Even today, Ed's home is just four blocks from his childhood home.

Ed has three brothers (John, Dave, and Glen) and two sisters (Lori and Marie). The children were born over a period spanning from 1958 to 1968. Murray had played Intermediate Hockey for the Simcoe Gunners when Intermediate Hockey was a very important game in Canada, and hockey would form an integral part of the family's upbringing. Brother John would play Junior Hockey. Dave went on to play NCAA Division One with the Rochester Institute of Technology (RIT) where he would tend goal as the team went on to win a National Championship. Ed, too, would go on to play Junior in Thorold. Glen would play up to Pee Wee before deciding that the game was not something that he wished to pursue further. Sister Lori played some hockey as well, while Marie's interests lay elsewhere. She was particularly fond of music, and played piano, an interest she inherited from Helen.

Murray was a big proponent of the family drawing life lessons from what he had learned while playing and coaching hockey. The Vince Lombardi quote that introduces this chapter, while coming from the world of football, was applied liberally in conjunction with hockey as he and Helen raised their brood. As Ed put it, most Catholic families such as theirs had a picture of The Last Supper on the wall. The Burkholders had the quote from Vince Lombardi. Not that Murray would ever try to force an interest in the game, though. He believed the kids should find their own interests in life, and he did his best to support them however he could. This is very much part of Ed's philosophy today.

The Burkholders were a close-knit family. The two sisters had their own bedroom, while the four boys shared the other bedroom on the second floor. The boys' room was nicknamed "the Barracks." During the heat of the summer, Murray would install one air conditioner in the boys' room and the girls moved their beds into the barracks. Six kids. One bedroom.

The family sat down to dinner together each night. Despite the preponderance of men in the family, the women held their own. Mom and dad saw to that. With both parents working to support the family, everyone shared in the responsibilities. The kids were expected to pitch in with dishes, laundry, and the like. They had to earn their way. Ed recalls that the four boys would have to clean their room. The two oldest (John and Dave) would sit on their beds and move the mess to the center of the room with their hockey sticks. The two youngest (Glen and Ed) would gather it together to put it all away or receive a disapproving tap from their older brother's hockey sticks.

Murray had one primary rule that the family had to follow. That was to make Helen's life as easy as possible. In return, he would always tell his kids that his wallet was always open to them if they helped around the house without having to be asked. Ed can recall that his father would provide a little "extra" if he were on his way out to the movies. Dad was always ready to reward them as best he could for doing the "little things" around the house. Ed remembers, at a very young age, helping his mother fold the laundry. With that complete, he went upstairs, only to return soon after to find Helen refolding everything. Still, she loved the extra effort.

The children shared just about everything. Ed only got his first pair of new skates in Grade 7. His first new bike came with his own money in Grade 12. Despite this, even the "hand-me-downs" felt new to him. With this came appreciation for everything they had in life. "Giving back" was a central tenet to life growing up. Once a week, the family would gather at Sunset Haven, a retirement home in the neighbourhood, and assist with a barbeque for the residents. Assisting others would continue to be a big part of Ed's life moving forward.

On his first day in Grade Four, Ed was headed home for lunch and was crossing Niagara Street in Welland when he was hit by a car. He somersaulted over the hood and landed on his head. He shook off the shock and walked home. A neighbour who was waiting in her car to pick up her child witnessed the accident and called Helen. Being a nurse, Helen immediately looked for signs of a concussion in her youngest child, including waking him every half hour that night. As time went on, it became apparent that Ed was having difficulties reading and writing. He was struggling at school. He was referred to the McMaster Medical Centre in Hamilton where he underwent an electroencephalogram (EEG) to monitor his brain activity. It was determined that there had been some brain damage, and Ed remained behind in Grade Four for a second year while he worked to regain skills such as basic reading and writing.

Immediately following the accident, Ed was also kept from playing the game he loved, Pee Wee AAA Hockey. He worked constantly on Murray and Helen so much, though, that they finally relented and allowed him to rejoin the team with his friends by Christmas. But a lot of hard work lay ahead as Ed not only continued to catch up during school hours, but to also put in extra work. Thanks to Helen's attention to detail (a quality he claims was passed on from her), she used her connections at Sunset Haven to get him some help by reading regularly with a resident there. Ever grateful to this day, Ed continued visiting with Mrs. Snodgrass until she passed away years later when he was twenty-one years of age.

Ed now looks back at the extra time in Grade Four as a blessing. One of his best friends, Mark Turner, was also held back that year. They were hockey teammates together and have remained close to this day. That year also allowed Ed to be aligned in school with his hockey teammates, which he credits with being even closer to them than he might otherwise have been.

Sunset Haven would also provide Ed with one of his earliest employment opportunities. For several summers he worked cutting grass and tending the gardens. To this day, he loves working in the garden. The "attention to detail" he inherited from his mother now gets focused into these efforts at his own home. In addition to the work at Sunset Haven, there was also part-time work while in school, cleaning carpets in industrial settings and private homes for a company known as Roto-Static.

As has already been noted, hockey was and still is a big part of life in Ed's family. One of the biggest honours for Ed was playing Midget AAA for the Gillespie Pontiacs in Welland. This was a team that was coached by Murray for several years prior to Ed joining them. He was the captain and a defenseman who not only loved to rush the puck, but also played with some "edge."

Ed recalls one game vividly. He picked up the puck in his own end and saw an opening that allowed him to take off, moving up the right side. As a left-hand shot, he was on his off-wing, and he made it as far as the hash marks in the Niagara Falls end. As such, he was running out of real estate and says now he should have put the puck on net. Instead, he continued to handle it and, in the process, took a heavy check while he was in an awkward position. As he picked himself up, he instantly knew something was terribly wrong. His left shoulder drooped dramatically, and he could not move his arm.

Managing to make it back to the bench, coach Lou Martineau suggested to Ed that he might have dislocated his shoulder and should get it checked out. At the first stoppage in play, he left for the dressing room, where he was met by Murray and the Junior team's trainer. They got his sweater and pads off to find his collar bone sticking out of his skin. His game was finished, and he was taken to the hospital by Murray, where the bone was set, Ed was fitted with a "crazy eight" brace and released. On the drive home, in great pain and unable to move very much, Ed listened as his father commented on the play which led to the injury. "You know Ed, you went into the corner wrong."

Ed can laugh about it today. But looking back, he knew his dad was concerned. First, because he would have to explain it to Helen, who never could go to watch the kids play hockey. It was too rough for her liking and this injury would just reinforce her feelings on the matter. But second, and perhaps most importantly, Ed spent the night sitting in a Lazy Boy chair in the basement. It was too uncomfortable to lie in bed. Murray spent the night with him sitting upright in a chair next to him. As Ed put it, "dad did not have to do that. I would have been fine down there on my own, but there was no doubting his fatherly concern and love after that."

Expressing one's feelings has always been a big part of life in the Burkholder family. He kissed his parents goodnight on their cheek daily until their deaths. Helen, too, insisted that the kids "hug it out" whenever the inevitable disagreements sprung up amongst themselves. Even today, Ed finds it difficult when he sees others suffer. As a result, philanthropy became a huge part of his life, and still is, to this very day. More on that later.

Ed lost his father to cancer in 1989. The disease was first diagnosed in a kidney, before progressing to his liver. Being a nurse, Helen arranged for a hospital bed to be moved into their home, where she would tend to all her husband's needs. This would include administering all the required meds.

Ed recalls that his father fought the disease with great dignity. He never complained. And while he had morphine available to him, Murray would never take it. As Ed put it, "I won't say that it was right or wrong not to take the medication available to him, but it was testimony to Murray's great strength and grace."

Mere months after Murray's cancer diagnosis, the family would be faced with more tough news. Helen was faced with a diagnosis of "viral cardiomyopathy." This is a condition of the heart caused by a viral infection causing myocarditis. This results in a thickening of the myocardium and dilation of the ventricles. The grim prognosis was that she might have as little as one year to live. In true Burkholder fashion, she would bravely battle through the continuing weakening of her heart until finally succumbing eighteen years later, in 2004.

Life for Ed continued to have its ups and downs. He was married to Lina (who he met while in high school) on September 22nd, 1990. Not long after, they had their first child, a son named Murray, for the grandfather he never had the opportunity to meet. It would take several years before they were blessed with the birth of their daughter, Emily Helen. Murray is now a teacher in Welland, and Emily has just completed her first year at McMaster University in Hamilton, where she studies psychology. Her uncle Dave jokes that Ed can be her first patient as she looks to become a therapist.

When Ed and Lina were in their sixth year of marriage, they would be faced with what was likely their biggest challenge up to that time. Ed began to experience pain in his left testicle. At first, he ignored it, likely out of some sense of embarrassment. But Lina, ever concerned, as Ed put it so eloquently, "ratted me out to my mother." As a nurse, Helen pressured Ed to see the doctor. She had one further request. Don't leave the office without a referral to a urologist. He did not know what a urologist was, but he promised her he would.

The first stop was the family doctors, a husband-and-wife team. She examined him first and then left the room while her husband checked things out. He then left the room, and she returned to explain that the hard-lump Ed felt was caused by a vein that was wrapped around the testicle. She suggested this was common in men his age and was nothing to be concerned with. She told him to go home and use ice to dull the discomfort. Then Ed remembered the promise to Helen, and he requested a referral to a urologist. This evoked a response of, "I just explained what the problem is. I will not give you the referral." Ever concerned with his promise, Ed explained that he could not leave without the referral. The doctor was annoyed, and asked, "Why?" "Because I promised my mother," he replied.

Perhaps seeing the futility of pursuing this further (or maybe she just needed the exam room for her next patient), Ed left with a referral to see Dr. Song. Within a week he was sent for an ultrasound. A week after that he met once again with Dr. Song, who explained he had a lump on the end of his left testicle. It might be cancer, but it might not. Either way, it had to come out.

Yet another week later, he had the testicle removed and was sent home. Just three weeks later, Ed was having extreme pain in his lower back. He walked the hall at night as he prayed for even a few moments of relief to catch his breath.

One evening while pacing the hallway, his brother John called the house. Lina answered and John asked her what the noise was in the background. Lina replied it was Ed and he was in great pain. John told her he would come right over. He called the hospital to tell them he was bringing his brother in. They told him they were already at capacity and not to come. But he ignored them and drove Ed right into the ambulance bay of the Emergency Entrance.

As soon as they saw Ed, he was admitted, and the subsequent examination discovered two tumors behind his abdominal wall. He had embryonal carcinoma. A few short days later he was starting a three and one-half-month regimen of high dose chemotherapy.

He could feel and taste every drop of the chemo treatment. He became extremely ill almost immediately. But within days of starting the treatments, the pain in his back disappeared. It would take continuing follow up visits to the doctor until January 2007 to be declared cancer-free. It is safe to say that the experience left an indelible mark on Ed for the rest of his life. I think it is also true that Ed drew on the strength demonstrated by Murray and Helen in dealing with their own health issues as he fought and won his own cancer battle.

Ed's life prior to the cancer diagnosis had followed a predictable route. An average student throughout high school, he graduated and then attended the Niagara College three-year business program. While math and accounting proved challenging, he excelled in the more creative realm of sales and marketing courses. Upon graduation, he followed in Murray's footsteps and was hired by London Life. He worked for them for two years selling RRSPs, life-insurance, and similar products. That experience led a hockey friend to suggest to Ed that he pursue a career in the automotive world.

from the world of sports or entertainment who would engage in lively discussion and debate. It primarily involved sports topics, and Landsberg was like an orchestra conductor encouraging his guests to be outgoing and opinionated.

Ed's first appearance saw him matched with former NHL Referee, Bryan Lewis. During the discussion concerning a particular interpretation of the rules, Bryan chose to make a point to Ed that he not only had a better understanding of the rules in question, but he also just happened to be carrying the rule book in his jacket pocket. Wanting to make a solid impression on national TV, Ed responded with, "I suppose you have the whistle in your other pocket." Landsberg loved it, making this the first of Ed's sixty-eight appearances on the show, landing him in the top three in appearances in the run of the show. He was also asked to appear on the final episode.

Just as "Off the Record" and his scouting work for the Red Wings were ending, Ed was faced with a dilemma. What would his next challenge be? He did not have to wait long. The Mississauga Ice Dogs were purchased by Bill and Denise Burke, and they planned to move the team to St. Catharines, Ontario. And with that, TV Cogeco was looking to televise their home games across Ontario via the OHL Action Pak on Cable TV. Producer Darren Sawyer was looking for a true hockey guy to be a colour commentator to analyze the action. He already had most of the on-air team assembled, and Steve Clark was lined up for play by play. (I had applied for the role of host.)

Darren had seen Ed on "Off the Record," and he liked what he saw. He called Ed to discuss the opportunity. But Ed was not certain he was right for the job. It took several discussions and one meeting with the four of us in Darren's TV Cogeco office to convince him. But once he was convinced, he was "all-in," as is typical for Ed. At the time of writing, we have become one of the longest standing on-air teams, broadcasting Ontario Hockey League (OHL) action for the past thirteen years.

When fans at home watch the games, many are struck by the "natural" chemistry Ed, Steve, and I seem to have. Mostly, this is a good thing. But there can be moments during a long season when it can lead us off the rails. One particularly memorable evening saw Ed and Steve on camera during an intermission. They were analyzing replays of goals scored and Ed was being his usual entertaining self, adding sound effects to his analysis. In and of itself, this was not unusual. But one effect led Steve to suggest that Ed had "reacted" to the pre-game chili in the media room. It struck Ed right in his funny bone and before long, the two of them were convulsed in laughter, unable to continue.

Meanwhile, in the production truck, producer Darren, not knowing whether to be angry with them or to laugh himself, had to throw from the two of them in the booth, to me at rink side—without warning. What people may not realize is that, normally while the two of them are on camera, I am often not tuned into their conversation as I am preparing for my next "on-camera hit." All I knew was that they were laughing uncontrollably as I scrambled to throw to the break, struggling not to laugh myself, even though I didn't know what the joke was. Overall, though, the four of us love working together, and each of us knows our role well.

Now in his early 50s, Ed Burkholder has, as you can see, led a full life. But there is another side to him that makes him want to give back. Ever grateful for all life has given him, he gives back to the world all that he has been given, and then some. I hinted earlier that he has become something of a philanthropist. His slogan, #Check Yourself Express Yourself...Everyone has a story, what's yours, is seen regularly on Facebook, Twitter, and Instagram in support of Cancer and Mental Health Issues. He reaches out to people who are dealing with various, often life-threatening, situations. Two such people were Julia Turner and Dalton Jacques.

Julia Turner was a teenaged woman who passed away from a cancerous brain tumor in 2011 in Welland. Every year since then, Ed and a committee host a pond-hockey tournament in a park near his home to raise funds and awareness for cancer research. It is known as Julia's Hope Cup, and hundreds come out in Julia's memory.

Dalton Jacques was a fifteen-year-old dealing with a rare form of bone cancer when he passed away in March of 2016. When Dalton came to his attention in the fall of 2015, Ed arranged for Dalton and his parents to attend an Ice Dogs Game as his guest. Dalton was treated to a tour of the team's dressing room, where he met the players, and was also introduced during our telecast. Just weeks before Dalton's untimely passing, Ed arranged for a bridge in downtown Welland to be lit with yellow lights in Dalton's honour. Hundreds of people came out in support, and the event was shared live with Dalton via video in his McMaster Hospital room in Hamilton.

Today, Ed is always working to help people through their cancer and mental health journeys by talking to them one on one. He also gives talks to schools, hockey teams, and in corporate settings. He always takes advantage of these talks to encourage young men, to "check their nuts," and not to be embarrassed to reach out for help. He is living proof this can save lives.

Today, Ed continues in the family tradition of running hockey skills clinics each summer with his son Murray. This was a tradition begun by his father Murray, and it continues today through his efforts. I asked Ed recently whether he believes in Destiny. Did he go through all his challenges in life so that he could give back? He answered with an emphatic "yes!"

I asked, when this chapter began, whether Murray and Helen Burkholder were aware of the impact their sixth child would have as he set out on his life journey in February of 1968. I would like to think that they are looking on from wherever they are, proud in the knowledge that he has turned all his life lessons into something profoundly better for all the lives he has touched.

CHAPTER THREE
Jim Thomson

"If nothing changes, nothing changes."

ALCOHOLICS ANONYMOUS

Jim Thomson would greet the world as an "almost" New Year's baby December 30, 1965. Born to Lyle Murray Thomson and Elizabeth Jean Thompson (yes, the spelling was different), he was the youngest of ten children when he arrived on the scene in Edmonton, Alberta. Lyle might just have been the best hockey player in Markham, Ontario. He was on the Boston Bruins' radar when his hockey career was derailed by his enlistment in the Infantry in 1942. Jean, as Jim's mother preferred to be called, grew up in England before moving to Canada following the War.

Jean had been in an earlier relationship, and she had five children prior to meeting and marrying Lyle in Penhold, Alberta. He worked as a chef in the oil fields of northern Alberta. He was responsible for providing three square meals a day for between 300 to 500 men, and would come home to Edmonton for the weekend, every second week. Together they would have four more children. The ten kids were all born between the mid-1940s and 1965.

Now if you are doing the math, you might note that totals nine kids. Years later when both parents had passed on and Jim was playing with the Los Angeles Kings, a daughter that Jean had had with, yet another father contacted one of Jim's sisters. It seems that Jean had escaped an abusive relationship with her first husband. She was told by the agencies responsible for providing financial aid that she would lose the children if she had any more kids. She decided therefore, to place this daughter, Noreen, up for adoption, and they never knew each other. When Jim finally met Noreen, he noticed an uncanny resemblance to Jean—their mother.

When he was six, in 1972, Jim and the family relocated from their apartment in Edmonton to the brand-new Westview Village mobile home park just outside Edmonton. They were in fact, the first family to move into what is now one of the largest mobile home parks in North America.

Lyle and Jean were both alcoholics. When Lyle was not working, he was drinking at home. Jean, too, had her addiction battles. Jim recalls she would get up in the morning and have a coffee. By 11:00 a.m., she would have a tea. At noon, she would begin drinking beer, and continue until she finished her day with a "Hot Toddy." She never had a driver's license and would hunker down at home most days. Jean had escaped a physically abusive relationship in Ontario to land in a verbally abusive relationship with Lyle in Alberta. Life in the trailer park was similar in many ways to that seen on the television show, "Trailer Park Boys."

The influence this lifestyle had on Jim was profound. He describes his parents as the best parents they could be while still being alcoholics. On the rare occasion he remembers visiting his father on the job, his most vivid memory was the large plastic tubs of ice cream in the giant freezers.

When he was nine, Jim's older brothers, John and Frank, bought a dairy farm. Jim spent that summer working seven days a week on the farm. This ended up having a profound impact on his work ethic.

Jim discovered the world of hockey at age six. He noted that while there was always enough money at home to satisfy the drinking and smoking habits of his parents, he would have to find his own way to pursue his new passion. A friend suggested that they go skating on one of the many ponds that surrounded the trailer park. Since Jim had no skates, the friend offered those of his father for Jim to try it out. There were no tendon guards on the back of the skates, but Jim took to it instantly. Other than crashing into snowbanks when it came time to stop, he was able to skate immediately, no doubt in no small part to the extra socks he put on to fill out the large man-sized skates.

Hockey followed a short time later. He went to Winterburn with his friends to try out for the Mite A team there. He had no gear and used borrowed skates. The coach began a drill where they would skate to the blue line and go down on both knees. They would get back up and skate to the red line and again go down on both knees, and once again get back up, only to repeat this at the far blue line. When the coach asked if Jim was wearing shin pads, Jim explained that he owned no gear. The coach immediately exempted him from continuing the drill. But six-year-old Jim did make the team.

People in the community banded together to get him second-hand equipment and raise the $180 Registration Fee. Jean and Lyle rarely, if ever, made it out to watch their son play. He relied on other parents to get him to and from the games, which were mostly played on outdoor rinks in the frigid Alberta winter. A particularly vivid memory for Jim was when they were hosting a team from nearby Warburg. It was snowing heavily, and the game went on anyway, on the outdoor ice. When the play went to one end of the ice, a few local fathers would leap over the boards to clear the ice before the play returned.

Of all the siblings, Jim and his sister Liz were the only siblings that got into sports. Despite her home situation, Liz somehow became a champion barrel racer and toured the Alberta Rodeo Circuit. Lyle, despite being an exceptionally talented hockey player himself would spend most days at home drinking with Jean rather than attend games. But Jim does remember attending a Winnipeg Jets and Edmonton Oilers World Hockey Association game with Lyle. What stuck out for Jim was being mesmerized by Winnipeg's Anders Hedberg, who scored three goals. From that time on, he was young Jim's favourite player, even when Anders left the WHA for the National Hockey League's New York Rangers. A particular memorable Christmas a few years later, saw Jim receive a Rangers Hedberg Jersey under the tree.

As has been noted, money to support Jim's hockey interest did not come easily. He remembers that Lyle would fill up the car at Esso when they had a promotion offering fifty-cent hockey sticks. Another memorable, if not, questionable, way to obtain sticks would be to go to the Parkland Arena when the men's league games were underway. Young Jim perfected the art of crawling along the boards to sneak away with one of the players extra sticks positioned at the end of the bench. It did not matter if it were curved left or right, because Jim would use the heat of the stove to curve the stick appropriately for him. He does not condone this action today. But as a child, he would do whatever he had to do to play.

By the time he was nine, Jim had a paper route that helped support his hockey interest. He remembers new skates and a hockey net as a couple of Christmas presents. Saturday nights meant Hockey Night in Canada with Bill Hewitt or Danny Gallivan. He would get into his pajamas while enjoying a root-beer float as he took in the games. But life was far from idyllic. His older brothers were bikers, and it was not unusual for young Jim to arrive home to thirty Harley-Davidson motorcycles surrounding their mobile home. As might be expected, he was exposed to some very unusual lifestyle choices at an early age. He was taught to physically stand up for himself, even though fighting was something, he was not fond of.

Perhaps it was the early influence of his older brothers, or it was choices made by Lyle and Jean, but young Jim would start down his own path into the world of addictions by the time he was twelve. The older brother of a friend would obtain bottles of sparkling wine called Baby Duck for them. Soon, every school day began with alcohol and marijuana.

As a student, Jim was anything but studious. He was addicted to hockey and spent his time in class perusing the Canadian Tire Catalogue sports section. By the time he was fourteen, his brothers took him with them to bars. With a hat on he could pass for someone old enough to drink. And when the inevitable bar room scraps broke out, Jim could hold his own, and he was taught to be sure to never get backed into a corner.

Meanwhile, his hockey career was starting to blossom. Memories of a best two out of three Pee Wee playoff series against Onoway stands out. After losing Game One, Jim recorded two assists in a 2-1 win in Game Two back on Home Ice. The third and deciding game was played in Onoway. Jim impressed spectators when he blasted a slapshot over the boards into the Zamboni entrance, and then got the lone goal in a 1-0 win.

The next series was against arch-rival Warburg. This was a rare occasion when Lyle and a friend attended Game One. Lyle's buddy offered Jim five dollars for every goal he scored. The young man more than rose to the challenge by scoring seven times and collecting thirty-five dollars. A small fortune by any standard in those days.

In Game Two, Lyle's friend could not be there, but he offered Jim the same deal, and once again, Jim responded with a seven-goal performance. As he rose through higher ranks of hockey, Jim became known more for his hardnosed, drop-the-gloves style of play. But in his younger years, he was offensively gifted, scoring sixty goals one season in Devon, Alberta.

At fourteen, Jim got his first taste of Junior Hockey. He was called up late in the season to play Junior B. He was playing with men who sported beards and were as old as twenty years of age. He recalls being unfazed, and he proceeded to score a goal. As his stick rose in celebration he was decked from behind by a defenseman on the other side. Jim jumped to his feet, dropped his gloves, and knocked the opposing player unconscious with one punch. And thus, the reputation as a tough guy was born.

His performance at age fourteen caught the eye of the Calgary Wranglers Major Junior Team. He got a tryout but did not earn himself a spot on their protected list. He returned home to continue his career in Midget. And more to the point, Jim would then begin to take his Hockey much more seriously. He told his mother that he wanted to drop out of school to focus on training and playing. At first, Jean would have none of it. But older brother Frank spoke to Jean and suggested she might as well allow him to do it. He would only do it anyway, despite her objections.

Once free of his schooling, Jim began to clean up his life. He stepped away from the alcohol and drugs. His brother helped him set up some weights at home to train, and he spent part of each day playing men's pick-up hockey at the Parkland Arena—using his own sticks this time. He did continue his education by enrolling in correspondence courses.

When he was fourteen, Lyle took Jim on his first plane ride to Markham to visit his Uncle Jim and Aunt Roma Regan. Uncle Jim asked Lyle to bring young Jim's skates. While he was there, his uncle had arranged for a try-out with the Markham Midget AAA Team, which included notables such as Steve Thomas. Steve would go on of course to a notable NHL career with the Toronto Maple Leafs.

While he was invited to join the team in Markham, Jim chose to return to Alberta to continue his career. Frank Bonello and Murray Titmarsh of the Toronto Marlboros Major Junior team flew to Alberta that winter to scout him. At the age of fifteen, Jim was invited to Camp with the Marlies. He lived in his uncle's basement in Markham, and while he did not immediately earn a spot on the Marlboros roster, he was assigned to their Junior A Farm team, the Markham Waxers. His first taste of Major Junior came during the playoffs. He joined the Marlboros, who had an offensively gifted lineup that included the likes of Steve Thomas and Peter Zezel. Their playoff opponents that year included the Cornwall Royals, led by Doug Gilmour.

The next season, young Jim joined the Marlies full time. It was a surreal experience moving from Westview Village mobile home park and playing on outdoor rinks to suiting up in Maple Leaf Gardens in Toronto. Jim recalls team owner Harold Ballard joining the team for the annual team photo. He insisted on his dog being in the picture, or he would not pose with the team. The photographer made a deal with Harold to take two photos. One with and one without the dog. I will leave it to your imagination as to which one became the official photo.

This was a star-studded team and, in a year where the Memorial Cup was going to be held in Ontario, Harold was eagerly anticipating being the host team, with its accompanying gate revenue. Jim remembers him during the team photo session, telling coach Tom Martin not to "F**k this up. Toronto needs this."

Fate was not kind to Harold and the team, though. In first place by a large margin at Christmas, the NHL's Philadelphia Flyers would take Peter Zezel, and the Boston Bruins would move Greg Johnston to "The Show" immediately after Christmas. There were few victories for the remainder of the Regular Season; the team finished second and made the Playoffs. The Kitchener Rangers hosted the Memorial Cup and the Ottawa 67's won it. Of note that year, Mario Lemieux played for the Quebec Major Junior Hockey League's representatives, the Laval Voisins.

In his first full season with Toronto, Jim recorded 10 goals, 18 assists, and 68 penalty minutes. Most of his time in the penalty box was made up of five-minute fighting penalties. Oddly enough, General Manager Frank Bonello did not want Jim back the next season. Uncle Jim made a deal with Frank to allow young Jim to attend camp at his expense. If he did not make the roster, his uncle would cover all the team's expenses. Jim knew nothing about this; he thought he was simply getting ready for the season. He made the team, and his uncle didn't tell Jim about it until years later. It was Head Coach Tom Martin's belief in Jim that led to his being drafted to the NHL.

When it came time for Draft Day, Jim was home in Westview Village. In those days, the first three Rounds of the Draft were on TSN Television. Jim's Agent, Rick Curran, suggested Jim could expect to be drafted anywhere from the third to the seventh round. Jean hosted a Draft Party at their mobile home, and everyone gathered around the TV. The first three Rounds came and went. TV coverage had ended and there was no social media providing updates. By dinner time, only Jim, Jean, and his best friend Dave Matthews were left at the party. Jim was devastated as the first seven Rounds came and went.

At 9:10 p.m. in Alberta (11:10 p.m. in the East where the Draft was taking place), Jean's pink rotary phone rang. It was Jack Button of the Washington Capitals calling to welcome him to their organization. Elation followed, as Jim saw his surreal NHL Dream coming true. He had talked to the Washington Capitals, Toronto Maple Leafs, and Winnipeg Jets. The Capitals took him in the ninth Round. The Capitals called Jim up to their American Hockey League (AHL) affiliate, the Binghamton Whalers. He saw limited action in four post-season games, recording no points and two penalty minutes.

The season following the Draft, Jim posted 23 goals and 51 points, while racking up 122 penalty minutes. There was no time in his life for drinking, drugs, or partying. To get to the Gardens from Markham, he would take public transit to the Finch Subway. On days when they practiced at Chesswood Arena, Uncle Jim would let him use his car. His uncle was a twenty-five-year recovering alcoholic and knew nothing about Jim's checkered past. All Jim would have to do was to think about partying, and he would be on the first plane back to Alberta.

Jim's first NHL Training Camp was in 1984. And it would be interrupted by sad news. He got a 3:00 a.m. phone call from his brother telling him that Lyle (who had been battling cancer) was not expected to live much longer. The team got him on a 6:00 a.m. flight and he got home in time to speak with Lyle just hours before he passed. He hung on long enough for Jim to get home and to say good-bye.

His first full season in the AHL was in 1985-86. In 59 games, he produced 15 goals, 24 points, and 195 penalty minutes. The leap from Junior to Pro was surreal for Jim. He was now expected to live as an adult. He shared a home with Grant Jennings (who was part of two Stanley Cup winners in Pittsburgh) and Yves Beaudoin. He was paid $1,372.46 every two weeks. When your rent is $125.00, a good steak was $4.00, and Busch Beer was $4.99 a case, it seemed like he was rich. They would practice in the mornings and go for chicken wings and beer in the afternoon. There was little to no emphasis on proper nutrition and fitness like there is today, other than ensuring that you had pasta as your pre-game meal.

It was during the 1986-87 season that Jim would get his first taste of NHL action. He was playing in the AHL with Binghamton, and the team was taking on the Hershey Bears in Hershey. Jim was given a special assignment to cover a 50-goal scorer by the name of Ross Fitzpatrick. His only job was to keep Ross off the scoresheet. There would be no fighting for Jim that weekend. By the time the weekend concluded on Sunday evening, Ross had been held to only two power-play assists in two games.

The management team of the Washington Capitals was on hand to watch those two games. As the Binghamton players emerged from the arena following the game on Sunday, the Brain Trust (including Washington Head Coach, Bryan Murray) were standing next to the team bus. Jim was called over to talk with them and his heart skipped a beat—he knew that meant he was about to be called up to "The Show."

Goaltending Coach Warren Strelow drove Jim to the Landover Maryland Marriot. He attended morning practice with the likes of Rod Langway, Mike Gartner, and Scott Stevens. Even though he had attended Training Camp with them, it was still special to be there getting ready to play with some of the league's great players.

Jim assumed he was there to fight. But he would get the surprise of his life when he met with Bryan Murray following practice. It seems that Management was so impressed by the job Jim had done covering Ross Fitzpatrick days earlier, he was going to be given even more responsibility. The Caps were hosting Mario Lemieux and the Pittsburgh Penguins. Jim's job (his only job) was to cover the great Mario Lemieux. When Bryan asked if he was nervous, Jim replied in the affirmative, but said he was excited to be given so much responsibility.

Game time arrived and things were going well. Jim stuck to Mario like glue. Frustrated, Mario even cross-checked Jim, and took a penalty. The Caps scored on the power play and Jim was practically giddy with the proceedings.

It would be short lived, though—during play a short time later, Kevin Hatcher and Kelly Miller broke out of the Caps end on a two on one. Jim, forgetting his instructions to stick with Mario, joined in to make it a three on one. Kevin "saucered" a pass to Jim only to see it fly over the Rookie's stick. Lemieux spun away with the puck on a breakaway. No goal resulted, but Jim knew his return to the bench would not be pleasant. Coach Murray let it be known in the loudest terms possible that Jim had only one job. And if he couldn't do it, Bryan would "bury him so deep into the minors that even the Hockey News wouldn't find him."

Years later after retirement from pro hockey, Jim attended an Ottawa Senators Game against the Penguins as a member of the team alumni. Mario, who was by that time an owner with the Penguins, was in a suite near the Senators Alumni suite. Jim knocked on the door and got to meet with the great Mario. He explained what had happened years earlier in Jim's first ever NHL Game. Mario did not remember Jim specifically, but he did remember the game in question because he was pissed off at Bryan Murray for the coverage he was subjected to. He was amazed that it was only Jim's first NHL game, and that he had been charged with covering one of the greatest players in hockey history.

Jim remained on the bench for the balance of the Pittsburgh game and stayed with the team for nine games before being returned to Binghamton. He had been injured fighting Mike Lawlor. Memories of walking into the Caps dressing room and seeing his jersey hanging there with his name on it remained etched in his mind as he worked to get back to the NHL. Still, life in the minor leagues was pretty good for Jim. Mark Taylor, who had played with Philadelphia and Pittsburgh, and Darryl Evans, who was famous for the Miracle on Manchester goal, were his mentors. Coach Larry Pleau became a father figure for him.

Around the time of the trade deadline in 1989, Clint Malarchuk (who would later almost die from a freak injury playing with the Buffalo Sabres) and Grant Ledyard were traded to the Buffalo organization. Jim and his team-mates gathered at Rod Langway's bar, which was known as Number 5, to wish them well. Jim, unsurprisingly, had a few too many and Langway drove him home. Upon arrival, his roommate, Mike Maillar, greeted him at the door. The Capitals General Manager David Poile had been calling looking for him. That meant he was being traded. So, he jumped in the shower to try and sober up before returning David's call.

When speaking to David, Jim learned he had been dealt to the Hartford Whalers Organization. He was to call GM Emile Francis right away. He would play the remainder of the season in Hartford, with Head Coach Larry Pleau. His stint with Hartford ended with a four-game sweep by the Montreal Canadiens during the playoffs.

He went on to score 25 goals and record 129 penalty minutes in 41 games with the Baltimore Skipjacks of the AHL, which was his most productive pro season. In the two years between 1988 and 1990, Jim saw action with the Washington Capitals (fourteen games), Hartford Whalers, the New Jersey Devils (3 games), and the Utica Devils (60 games). He scored 21 goals and 44 points, along with 124 penalty minutes, for Utica.

New Jersey called him up. It seems they were going to play in Toronto on a Saturday night and Jim was to have an appointment to fight their tough guy, John Kordic. The game would be seen nationally in Canada on Hockey Night in Canada. Before Saturday arrived though, the Devils talked Troy Crowder out of retirement, and he fought Kordic.

Jim's coach in Utica was Tom McVie, who he described as the best coach he ever played for. Upon his arrival with the Devils, Jim had dinner with Tom. Tom asked Jim if still wanted to play in the NHL. The reply was, of course, a definitive yes. At this point, Tom asked Jim his playing weight. When Jim replied, "220 pounds," McVie suggested that he would have to get down to 212 pounds or he would never see the ice in Utica, let alone New Jersey. After much time in saunas and the gym for the next week or so, Jim got down to the required weight.

Throughout Jim's career, his path to the Pros was defined primarily by one thing. His ability and willingness to fight, despite showing he had offensive abilities during his younger years. Looking back, he regrets this part of his hockey career. In those days, virtually every NHL team had at least one and sometimes two "enforcers" in their lineup. Their sole role was to instill fear into the other team.

As noted earlier, Jim hated fighting. It produced considerable stress and anxiety and played a role in his rapidly developing alcohol and drug addiction. Years later, when he spoke out about how all this made him feel, Don Cherry and some former NHL enforcers would call him out as a puke, hypocrite, and a turncoat during a Hockey Night in Canada's "Coaches Corner" segment. They suggested he had benefitted from his days as an enforcer, and by suggesting that fighting should be removed from the game, he was out to cost them their jobs.

Jim defended himself, though. He said he was only speaking for himself, contending that the fighting and subsequent substance abuse, eight concussions, and other injuries almost cost him his life. He intends to submit his brain for study, looking for signs of Chronic Traumatic Encephalopathy (CTE), when he eventually dies. He notes that enforcers such as Bob Probert, Rick Rypien, Derek Boogaard, and other "enforcers" are overly represented in deaths due to suicide, early onset dementia, anxiety and depression diagnoses, drug and alcohol addictions, and other chronic nagging health issues. To this day, Jim suffers from constant ringing in his right ear.

Jim notes that fighting is now all but removed from Junior Hockey. Players must be able to contribute hockey skills to play. Years later while filming a Mike Myers hockey comedy, Love Guru, both he and Bob Probert got to share some time together. Both agreed that when they were told ahead of time that they would be fighting in an upcoming game with the other team's tough guy, it produced incredible anxiety. They felt that there was always somebody coming for them, and that they were one lost fight or injury away from ending their career.

Jim is not part of the ongoing concussion related lawsuit being led by Daniel Carcillo and other former NHL players against the NHL. He feels that while they all have a right to their platform, he knew what he was getting into, and he has chosen not to take part. In his first season of pro hockey in Binghamton, he incurred 195 minutes in penalties. The Capitals suggested that if he ever wanted to play in the NHL, he would have to fight more. And fight he did. The next year in Binghamton, he fought 41 times and racked up 360 minutes in the penalty box. By season's end, he had to have surgery on his hand because of all the fighting.

Not all experiences in Jim's career were negative, though. By 1990, he was a Free Agent and in discussions with several NHL teams for his services. It came down to signing a deal with the Detroit Red Wings. Bob Probert was no longer with them, and they were shopping for the services of someone such as Jim. He was about to sign the deal when his Agent mentioned that the LA Kings were willing to match the Detroit offer, but he did not recommend signing with LA. They already had Marty McSorley, Jay Miller, and others, so he would likely be sent to the minors.

Jim did not accept the advice though. The Kings had the Great One, Wayne Gretzky, and several other former Edmonton Oilers in their lineup. This was a powerful motivator as he had grown up watching and cheering for his hometown Oilers. He instructed his representative to accept the Kings offer; he would find a way to make the lineup.

He began the season as predicted, with the Kings AHL affiliate, the New Haven Nighthawks, where he played twenty-seven games and spent 121 minutes in the penalty box. He was getting $40,000 for the season in New Haven and would get $190,000 for making the Kings. Jim's dream of playing with his idol, Wayne Gretzky, became a reality late in the season when he was called up for the last eight games of the regular season and the playoffs. In 1991/92, he saw action in forty-five Kings games, scoring once and incurring 162 minutes in penalties.

Jim has some vivid memories of playing with and being around the Great One (Wayne Gretzky). His time in the NHL began with Mario Lemieux, and it now included Gretzky. During the opening round of the Stanley Cup Playoffs in Calgary, Wayne invited a group of players, including Jim, to join him at a Calgary restaurant for dinner. They won the next game and Wayne made sure the same group dined together for the duration of their playoff run. Jim was always grateful for the appreciation Wayne had for those, such as himself, who were there to help protect him.

That playoff run in LA took the club to the finals against the Montreal Canadiens (the Habs). Along the way, Gretzky famously got away with a high stick on Toronto's Doug Gilmour in the Western Conference finals, and Leaf fans contend to this day that it cost them a chance to play the Habs. As Jim noted, there are two sets of rules. One for the superstars and one for everyone else. This is not only true in hockey, but in life.

Jim was known as something of a practical joker throughout his career. When the team was in Montreal for the finals, they won Game One. In Game Two, they were leading after two periods, and during the second intermission, Gretzky told the team if they won that game, they would sweep the Habs in four straight games back in LA.

Fate it seemed, had a different plan. Montreal stormed back following a famous incident initiated by Habs Coach Jacques Demers, with 1:24 to go in the third period. He requested a measurement of Marty McSorley's illegally curved stick, which led to a Kings penalty. Montreal was able to even the score on the ensuing power play and go on to defeat the Kings during overtime. In the LA room following the game, players were showering and getting dressed, and Gretzky was being summoned to meet the throng of reporters to comment on the loss. Dressed only in his underwear, shoes, and socks, the Great One turned on the hair dryer, only to find himself and the entire room covered in a cloud of baby powder. He emerged white from head to toe only to exclaim, "Jim. NOW is NOT the Time," as he returned to have another shower. Jim does not admit responsibility to this day, though.

LA brought Jim into contact with a host of unusual and mostly famous people. Bruce McNall had bought the LA Kings and traded for the Great One with Edmonton owner Peter Pocklington. Jim will not comment on McNall's eventual legal troubles, but he does say that he was treated unbelievably well by Bruce. And through Bruce, the team was surrounded by people such as actors John Candy and Alan Thicke. Self-help guru Anthony Robbins travelled with them and gave them pep talks.

The Head Coach, Barry Melrose, was a "grinder" during his playing days and he appreciated the role that players such as Jim played on a team. In fact, LA would lose Jim to the Ottawa Senators during the Expansion Draft, only to get him back because Wayne Gretzky asked Barry to arrange it. Pretty heady company for a kid from Westview Village Trailer Park.

Jim rounded out his pro hockey career from 1991 to 1994 with brief stops in Phoenix (IHL), Ottawa (NHL), LA (NHL), and the Anaheim Mighty Ducks (NHL). During his first game with the Ducks, he injured his shoulder. He played through the pain for five more games before having three surgeries and going through rehab. Eventually, Anaheim bought out the remainder of his deal and his hockey career was done. He had just turned twenty-seven years of age.

Jim awoke the morning following his release from Anaheim, and he lay there thinking that, for the first time in his adult life, he was no longer special due to being a pro athlete. He would have to adjust to being a "normal" human being. He had married his high school sweetheart, Sue, while playing in Binghamton. He had broken off the engagement during his first season there, because he felt too young for so much responsibility. But one night while the team was playing in Rochester, teammates Darryl Evans and Mark Taylor told Jim that Sue had called looking for him. Not realizing that he was being pranked, he got her on the phone. Of course, she wanted to know why he was calling, and after they realized what had happened, they started talking. They not only got back together; they were married that summer.

Jim and Sue had three children together. Now adults, daughter Emma is a real estate agent, son James is a hockey player at Wilfred Laurier University in Waterloo, Ontario, and son Jonathon is a field lacrosse player attending college in Ohio. As anyone who has retired knows, it can be a daunting experience, even for someone who is much older than Jim was. At twenty-seven years of age, retirement was positively paralyzing.

The couple returned from Anaheim California and moved in with Sue's parents in Unionville, Ontario. Jim's addictions took on a new life—he smoked more dope, drank more alcohol, and graduated to using crack cocaine and OxyContin. He had gotten a job and found a cocaine buddy who kept him supplied.

At his lowest point, Jim went so far as to alter an Oxy prescription from 15 pills to 150. This of course, is considered indictable and almost led to his being arrested, along with the ensuing news stories and effects on his young family that would have followed.

This went on for several years until one day his best friend Richard told him he wanted to see Jim at 9:00 a.m. the next morning. This oddly specific request seemed unusual to Jim, but he went anyway. He arrived at the house to find not only his buddy, but his wife Sue, her parents, his cousin, and another friend, Shawn Sheppard, all there. They staged an intervention, and they all read letters explaining that they loved him and telling him that he was destroying his life and that of his family and friends. From there, he got into a friend's truck and was taken to a rehab Centre in Merrickville, Ontario, near Ottawa.

For the first time in Jim's life, he was getting professional help with his addictions. If he had not had that help, he admits he likely would have died from suicide, if not a heart attack. For the first two weeks, Jim was not allowed contact with anyone outside of the facility. He was in class all day every day to work on relationship and life skills, in addition to working on his addiction. At that point, he was visited by Sue, his mother-in-law, and the kids. In a meeting with Sue and his counsellor (Brian) after lunch, he listened as Sue poured out all her anger and frustration. She wanted a divorce.

Jim did not see that coming, and after the family left and Jim had finished dinner, Brian called him into his office. He asked Jim directly if he could see a life for himself with Sue. Broken-hearted, he admitted that he could not. Several weeks later, after being released from rehab, Jim returned home. Sue and the kids were not there, having left on a four-day trip to the Dominican Republic. Jim was originally supposed to be with them, but now it was time for him to gather up his belongings and move out.

Unbelievably, Jim had not yet hit rock bottom. He still, on three occasions, considered taking his own life. Before the intervention, he would lie in bed at night feeling high and afraid to even move his leg because it made him feel as though he would have a heart attack. The NHL Players Association played a part in his getting treatment in Merrickville, but now he was back on his own and struggling to stay sober.

One evening he was on a date with a lady he had met. They went to The Keg Steakhouse, and knowing nothing about Jim's situation, she ordered a nine-ounce glass of Kendall Jackson Chardonnay. As fate would have it, prior to his treatment, this had been a drink of choice for him. Trying to stay sober, he ordered soda water, but she would have none of it. She insisted he join her in a glass of wine, and he accommodated her, ordering his own Chardonnay.

He had a second glass with dinner, and upon returning home that evening, he called his drug dealer. This continued until November 17, 2007. Jim had made a business trip to Edmonton for a public relations job. While there, he went on a forty-eight-hour bender, partying non-stop. At the conclusion of the trip, he boarded his Toronto-bound flight hung over and exhausted. He was sweating profusely, to the point that a woman seated next to him asked if he was all right. He explained that he was okay and was simply recovering from forty-eight hours of non-stop partying. He then closed his eyes, and thoughts of what his life had become flooded his mind.

He now knew he could not go on like this. Quietly, he surrendered to his sobriety. Upon arrival at home, he quietly and unceremoniously threw out all the booze and drugs in the house. For him, one drink was too many and one hundred not enough. He thought about his rehab counsellor, Brian, who had explained to him that his only job was to stay sober. If he could do that, little gifts would "fall from the sky." As of this writing, that was twelve years ago, and he has been sober ever since.

The first of those "little gifts" was the arrival of the woman in his life, who is now his wife. Rita is a woman of strong religious faith, and she and Jim started attending church together. For the second time in his life, Jim surrendered himself to a higher purpose. He had not experienced religion while growing up. One time at his uncle's home in Markham, he emerged from his room in the basement to find his Aunt Roma and several of her Catholic Church friends sitting and chatting. When one asked him what faith he was, he replied "Pedestrian." This drew some polite chuckles from the ladies, who suggested that he meant "Protestant."

Today, Jim spends his days "giving back" in several ways. He stages interventions for fellow addicts in the basement office in his home. Surrounded by hockey memorabilia, those being helped gravitate to and identify with his days as a pro athlete. Often Jim drives these people to treatment programs such as the one he underwent in Merrickville.

He also gives talks at homeless shelters. When he is about to begin these PowerPoint presentations, he tells those in attendance that they are about to see and hear stories about Gretzky, Lemieux, and life as a professional athlete. But he also explains that this life did not make him immune to many of the same problems they face on the streets in their own lives. He does not judge anyone, and he feels that if he only reaches one person there, then his time will have been well spent.

In addition, Jim is now the proud owner of the Aurora Tigers Junior A team. They are located just north of Toronto and play in the Ontario Junior Hockey League (OJHL). Every summer, he stages a seven-week program of mentoring and training for elite players that he calls the "Boys of Summer" and the "Endless Summer." Jim has been running these hockey schools for over twenty years now.

All of Jim's life experiences caught the attention of TSN's Michael Landsberg, the host of the long running show "Off the Record." The show is no longer on the air, but Jim was a guest on ninety-two occasions, second only to former NHL Player, Ric Nattress, who had ninety-five appearances. Jim loved being on the show but hated it when the three guests would talk over each other.

Now in his fifties, Jim can look back with pride at all he has achieved. He hit rock bottom in November of 2007 to emerge healthier and happier than ever. Other than the births of his kids, his favourite memory is the moment of "surrender" during that Air Canada Flight. It has given him all that he now has, a solid marriage, a great family, and a purposeful life helping others. He now lives an honest, sober existence, and he no longer worries about juggling a life of lies fearing that his faults may suddenly be revealed to all.

As they say in Alcoholics Anonymous, "If nothing changes, nothing changes."

CHAPTER FOUR
Mike Farwell

"A person who has the ability to help others and fails to do so, has wasted their life."

ROBERTO CLEMENTE

Former Major League Baseball Player
and Humanitarian

Mike Farwell entered the world in August of 1971 in Kitchener Ontario about ninety minutes west of Toronto. He was the third child born to Bernie and Marianne Farwell. Eventually there would be five children. Brother Tom arrived in 1968, and sisters Luanne in 1969, Pam in 1973, and the youngest, Sheri, who was born in 1975.

To everyone outside of the family, everything appeared to be normal; that is, until Luanne turned five and was diagnosed with Cystic Fibrosis (CF). Similarly, Sheri was diagnosed with CF at birth. For a child to be afflicted with CF, both parents must carry a specific defective gene. And even then, the odds are one in four that that they would have such a child. For the Farwells, two of their five children were affected, despite having no previous family history.

According to the Cystic Fibrosis Canada website:

CF is the most common fatal genetic disease affecting Canadian children and young adults. At present, there is no cure. One in every 3,600 children born in Canada have CF. It mainly affects the digestive system and the lungs.

Typical complications include:

- Difficulty digesting fats and proteins
- Malnutrition and vitamin deficiencies because of inability to absorb nutrients
- Progressive lung damage from chronic infections and aberrant inflammation
- CF-related diabetes
- Sinus infections

To anyone who did not know of Luanne and Sheri's CF, nobody would think that they were afflicted by a life-threatening illness. Along with their siblings, they led the same busy lives as most middle-class Canadian kids, the only outward sign being a cough, which only those familiar with CF might recognize.

Twice daily percussion treatments were performed by Bernie. These twenty-minute treatments consisted of lying on a folding table, alternating between lying face down and face up, with dad operating a trigger that allowed a type of hammer to thump on their chest and back. These treatments normally occurred prior to breakfast and again prior to dinner. The object of the treatment was to loosen the mucus in the lungs. Bernie would watch a business channel on TV as he performed the procedure. As the girls got older and could assist, dad would sometimes be able to perform this on both sisters simultaneously. On some occasions, the other children in family would help. When they ever went on vacation in the family station wagon, all this equipment was transported in a roof-top wooden box, specifically built by dad.

In addition to percussion, there was also a fifteen-minute treatment during which Luanne and Sheri wore a mask that dispensed a mist that they would breathe into their lungs. They also took thirty or more pills containing enzymes with every meal—these assisted with breaking down the mucus in their lungs and digestive tracts.

While all this took place each day, Tom, Mike, and Pam never thought much about it. These treatments were just part of everyday life at the Farwells. The percussion treatments tended to be loud, and the other kids might sometimes complain that they could not hear a show they were watching on TV. Otherwise, it was just business as usual.

Twice a year, Luanne and Sheri required check-ups at Toronto's Hospital for Sick Children (Sick Kids). The whole family piled into the family station wagon to make the trip. Eventually, Grand River Hospital (now known as Kitchener-Waterloo Hospital) started a clinic and would take over these check-ups. This meant no longer having to devote an entire day to travel the ninety-minutes each way to Toronto.

When the girls were growing up, the average lifespan for someone with CF was twenty-four years. That fact was something Mike never really considered as a child. But, looking back he feels the girls were aware and as such, tried to fill their lives with as much living as possible.

Luanne passed away in 1993. She was just twenty-four, and as Mike recalls, was pretty much a classic text-book case. She declined slowly until near the end. At age sixteen, she approached Bernie and Marianne with a very specific request. She loved children and wanted to quit school to concentrate on her passion of babysitting kids in the neighbourhood. She felt she would never have children of her own and was seemingly aware her time would be short.

Despite Bernie being a schoolteacher, her parents agreed to support her desire. She would get up at six a.m. most days and she filled her days, until well into the evening, looking after local kids. Mike recalls a photo in the newspaper of Luanne surrounded by what seemed like two dozen kids she looked after. The picture was accompanied by an article that described her and her passion.

While Luanne was considered typical of CF cases, Sheri was another matter. She passed away suddenly, and somewhat unexpectedly, at age eighteen, just nine short months after her sister. Mike recalls her as very active and the life of the party. Being physically active is considered very important for those with CF. And Sheri took this very much to heart, filling her days playing baseball and basketball.

Until he lost his sisters, Mike had led a pretty typical life, similar to that of most middle-class Canadian kids. He was a baseball fan and would have liked to play. But, by his own admission, he was a little chubby growing up and his parents felt he should be more active. So instead, he played a little soccer. He played a limited amount of hockey, but he was not a great skater, so he stuck primarily to street hockey.

As a student, he was good enough to stay out of trouble with the teacher in the family. He attended the University of Waterloo as an English and History Major and followed Bernie into the family business as a teacher. But, about halfway through his first year he recognized that he did not have a "fire in his belly" for the profession. As he says, "God bless my father for wanting to do it all those years. It just wasn't for me."

He had watched WKRP in Cincinnati on TV growing up and thought Johnny Fever pretty much had the coolest job on the planet. Like his favourite TV character, Mike wanted to be on the radio. He wasn't sure it was even a "real" job like teaching, but he sat down with Bernie, despite being terrified to tell him.

Happily, for Mike, his dad told him to chase his dream, and that he would always support him. So, he went off to study broadcasting at Conestoga College in Kitchener. By June of 1995, he was working part-time in nearby Brantford, Ontario at CKPC AM and FM, hosting the overnight show on weekends.

Full-time work followed in the summer of 1996. He moved just about as far west as one could get in Canada, to Salmon Arm, British Columbia. Making $17,200 a year, he was a DJ playing "Today's Best Music" on Saturday and Sunday mornings from six a.m. to noon, and Monday and Tuesday evenings from six p.m. to midnight. On Fridays he performed whatever duties the station required.

While he was spinning the tunes of Celine Dion and Elton John in Salmon Arm, he knew he wanted something different, and he wrote to a childhood idol back in Kitchener. Don Cameron was the radio voice of the Kitchener Rangers Ontario Hockey League team for decades and Mike grew up listening to him. He explained to Don that someday he would like to have a job like his.

Mike was thrilled when Don wrote back, encouraging him to get as much experience as possible while continuing to pursue his dream. And Mike took it to heart as he moved into news with a station in Thunder Bay, Ontario. Then it was back to his hometown, Kitchener, where in addition to radio, he joined Rogers TV as host of the telecasts featuring the Ontario Hockey League's Guelph Storm in 2000 and 2001. He eventually became the colour analyst in Guelph before Rogers moved him to host the Kitchener Rangers telecasts.

Over time, he did colour commentary, and then finally, play by play, on TV in Kitchener. A few years later, he got the opportunity to move to the role of colour commentator on the radio, covering the Kitchener Rangers, with his lifelong idol, Don Cameron, doing play by play. He recalls being "weak-in-the-knees" immediately prior to his first game with Don in Windsor.

His dream of working with Don would be complete when Don retired a short time later, after a career of fifty years. Since then, Mike has had the honour of following in Don's footsteps as his play-by play successor.

Mike continues to work full-time for Kitchener's 570 News (now known as CITY News 570) as a weekday talk show host from nine to noon at AM 570. He also did a brief stint with Sportsnet 590 The Fan in Toronto, doing sports updates and co-hosting the morning show. Today he divides his time between talk show host and hockey play-by-play.

When Mike lost his sisters, he was in his early twenties. His family were practicing Catholics and as he grew up, they attended Mass every Saturday evening at 7:15. This made it tough for them to get home for the start of Hockey Night in Canada on TV. But once there, he often turned the volume off and did his own play by play.

After his sisters were gone, Mike felt lost and angry. He looked at the other families in the close-knit local CF community and wondered why they had kids who survived and the Farwells did not. He felt increasingly isolated from his Catholic faith, and he felt he needed to do something about CF.

He was just launching his broadcasting career and was unsure how he could contribute to the cause. At first, he was fully prepared to jump headfirst into becoming the President of the local Chapter in Kitchener-Waterloo (K-W). Bernie intervened, though. He had spent years working with the local chapter and knew the demands it would bring. He also knew the burning desire

Mike felt was likely the grief speaking. So, he convinced his son to take a step back and let things unfold naturally while he got his new career and life off the ground.

Still, Mike wanted to do something. What skills could he call on to contribute? The thing that jumped out at him was that he was good at speaking. He thought, what if he offered to be Master of Ceremonies (MC) at the Annual "Walk to Make CF History." He made the offer to the CF Chapter, and they happily accepted. After all, not everyone was comfortable speaking in front of people and Mike was something of a celebrity now, being on the radio in K-W, having returned from his earlier broadcasting stops across Canada.

Mike not only was the MC, but he also participated in the Walk and got some pledges on his own. His boss at the Station allowed him to do some limited promotion of the event on air. At no time though, did he reveal his own history with CF publicly. This was personal and he felt no one would be interested in the "gloomy" details. Besides, even though he was a radio host by profession, he was (oddly enough) an introvert by nature.

Mike's boss at CITY News 570 knew of his personal connection to CF, and after a year or two as the MC of the local walk, spoke with him about it. He felt that Mike's impact could be even greater if he let people know his family's story. He would need to tell "his" story—he would need to do what he got people to do every day on the radio, which was to personalize things so that listeners would have a more personal connection.

It took a while to convince him, but Mike was slowly coming around to the idea. Still, he was unsure how to go about it. Once again, he thought back to watching WKRP while growing up. What if he were to engage in a stunt or stunts to raise money? Radio hosts historically had done such things as sitting atop a billboard for a week or riding a Ferris wheel for two weeks.

Mike had no plan, but he quickly came up with a list of things he would do. He allowed people to pay to throw softballs at him in a dunk tank in Waterloo's Public Square. He boxed three rounds with professional boxer "Fitz the Whip" Vanderpool while the crowd chanted "one more round." He and a group of friends also jumped out of a plane. By the time he was finished that year, he had raised approximately nine thousand dollars.

The year prior to doing the stunts, Mike had raised around two thousand dollars by getting people to sponsor him in the "Walk." He had now increased that to nine thousand. How could he increase it even more the following year? He might be an introvert by nature, but by his own admission, he was a "competitive introvert." He felt compelled to create a better outcome for those with CF and their families than he and his family had. He also felt awkward returning year after year to ask the same people to support him with donations.

Slowly an idea began to form—he could perform a task and get paid with a donation. He approached the local CF folks and asked them what they thought. They thought he might be on to something. With the support of his boss at CITY News 570, he could generate a lot of publicity and potentially raise a lot of money for the cause. What was needed next, they felt, was a formal business plan, and they needed to consult with their lawyers to come up with waivers and liability insurance.

At his point, Mike felt he was on different trajectory. He had come this far with no formal plan and was not inclined to get the lawyers involved. Thus, he decided to move ahead on his own. With limited radio exposure, he promoted himself on social media such as Facebook and Twitter. Any liability would be "on him."

He started offering his services doing whatever jobs people needed doing in return for a donation. These tasks could be anything from weeding gardens, washing cars or cleaning gutters. The campaign ran for the month of May to coincide with CF Awareness Month. It concluded on the final Sunday of May when he would turn over any funds, he raised at the CF Walk. He promoted each job he did on social media.

Every day when his shift at 570 News was over, he went out and did four or five jobs. That first-year, he weeded many gardens, which is something he personally hates doing. By the day of the CF Walk, there were still a few outstanding requests for him to work for donations, so he extended his efforts one additional week, finishing at the end of May. His efforts netted CF around twenty thousand dollars.

To date, there have been seven annual Farwell-4-Hire Campaigns, as they have come to be known. He has done a lot of different jobs, including serving coffee in Tim Hortons and ice cream at Dairy Queen. He has driven a rolling machine to smooth asphalt and operated a machine crushing scrap cars in a wrecking yard.

Perhaps the most unique job he ever did was to clean the sheath of a horse. Without going into detail, this involves wearing a latex glove, using some lubricant such as K-Y gel and inserting the gloved hand into the rear end of the horse to clean the pouch containing the genitalia. The horse was named Bailey and Mike says they still talk at least once a week!

For the most part, the jobs Mike performs during each campaign are in the immediate area of Waterloo Region. One year though, Steve Fitsimmons, who is the TV play-by-play voice of the Guelph Storm and a college buddy of Mike's, asked him to come on a telecast to promote the Campaign. When the interview was over, Mike got a few requests from different parts of Ontario to perform jobs in their area. One came from Ottawa (a six-hour drive from Kitchener) to come and clean their gutters. The caveat was that he would have to rent scaffolding. Mike politely declined, explaining that it was not only too far away, but would be too expensive to rent the scaffolding.

Mike dreamed of the time when he could raise one hundred thousand dollars in a single campaign. The year that was achieved was extremely satisfying, but also a little frightening. Would he be able to continue achieving that level of support? Things had grown more than he had ever dreamed possible. But now, the folks at CF were accustomed to such support, and were coming to count on it each year.

He need not have been concerned though. During the campaign in 2020, he raised one hundred and fifty-six thousand dollars despite the Covid-19 pandemic. He made accommodations such as doing no indoor events and extending the campaign to the end of June.

To date, Mike has managed to increase the amount raised each year and in seven years has raised a total of more than five hundred thousand dollars through his efforts. In short, life is good for Mike and his family. He gets to work in his chosen profession of radio broadcasting. He is happily married to his wife of six years, Jennifer, and they live in Kitchener with his teen-aged stepdaughter, Kayley. He also has an adult son, Steve, from a previous relationship.

When not on the radio or raising support for CF, he enjoys a coffee and crossword on Sunday mornings. He is an avid motorcyclist and is often found (weather permitting) on his Kawasaki Ninja. He loves the sport-touring bike and still does not feel grown up enough to ride a cruiser.

As mentioned previously, when Mike lost his sisters, the average life expectancy for those with CF was twenty-four years. Today, thanks to the support of those like Mike, that life expectancy is now fifty years. Percussion treatments no longer involve manually pulling a trigger; there is now a vest that CF patients can wear to automatically perform this task. And the number of enzyme pills consumed at each meal has been dramatically reduced.

Mike describes himself as "The Accidental Fundraiser." Looking back at the years since losing Luanne and Sheri, he takes great satisfaction in having contributed to the advancements described here. He is happy that he has been able to connect with many of the same CF patients and their families that he has known most of his life.

Beyond improving lives, Mike prefers to think in terms of finding a cure for Cystic Fibrosis. He truly believes this is possible. He is also glad now that Bernie urged him not to jump right into the affairs of the local CF Chapter when his sisters passed away. He took his time and slowly found his best way to lend his support. He is no longer hesitant to share his story and is grateful to his boss for convincing him to do so many years ago. He is impressed by the hundreds of people he meets every year during his campaigns, people like Sam and her husband Tiago, who volunteered their services to increase his presence on social media and created the logo for "Farwell-4-Hire."

Perhaps the biggest push Mike needed to make all this happen came when he was much younger, reading a biography of the late Roberto Clemente. He was a Major League Baseball all-star who played for the Pittsburgh Pirates in the 1960s. He was a Latin American by birth and never forgot his humble beginnings. He used his fame to raise support and awareness for the poverty where he was from. He died in a plane crash at age thirty-eight in 1972 while on a flight carrying supplies back to his home country. A quote from Roberto in the book has stuck with Mike ever since.

"A person who has the ability to help others and fails to do so, has wasted their life."

There probably is not a better way to sum up Mike's life!

CHAPTER FIVE

Ben Fanelli

"Decide to be the hero of your story."

BEN FANELLI – HEROIC MINDS

Thursday October 30th 2009, was typical of most nights in an Ontario Hockey League (OHL) season. The Major Junior Hockey League had conducted its business of developing young hockey talent for professional leagues around the world, including the National Hockey League (NHL).

Four games were played that evening. One saw the Kitchener Rangers take on the Brampton Battalion at Brampton's Powerade Centre. For sixteen-year-old rookie defenseman Ben Fanelli, it was just his fourth game in what was to be a promising Junior career. It was a satisfying effort, both for Ben and the team as they shut out the Battalion 4-0. Ben put no points on the board that evening, but he was on the ice for one of Kitchener's four goals to finish plus one on his plus/minus rating. He chatted happily with his parents (Sue and Frank Fanelli) and brother (Chris) while waiting to board the team bus for the trip back to Kitchener. They had made the forty-minute drive from nearby Oakville to take in the game. All in all, it was an effort the rookie was proud of.

It was time to go, so Ben hugged his family and boarded the bus to perform his rookie duty passing out food to his hungry teammates on the bus. They headed back to Kitchener the forty-five-minute drive to where they would prepare for their next game the following evening when they would host fellow Western Conference rivals, the Erie Otters.

The next thing Ben remembers was opening his eyes. He lay in a Hamilton hospital bed with his mother standing to his left and a doctor to his right. Sue asked if he knew why he was there. He had no answer, as he did a mental inventory of his limbs to see what he had broken. Instantly he teared up and thought that he had no pain. So then, why was he there?

The doctor took over the conversation. In the game against Erie, he was hit by another player, and his face was driven into one of the metal stanchions that held the glass in place. He was taken off the ice, unconscious and on a stretcher, and rushed to the hospital in Kitchener. From there, he was transferred by helicopter to Hamilton General.

The doctor wasted no time in getting to the heart of the matter. Ben had been in an induced coma and was only now being brought out of it. He had three bleeds on his brain. One on the surface and two inside. He would not be able to participate in sports for the rest of his life. There would be no school for at least two years, and when he was able to resume, he would likely require a teaching assistant. In short, life would be very different than it had been for his first sixteen years.

Ben spent seven days in hospital as he and his family contemplated the possibility that he might need brain surgery. As the week in hospital wound down, the possibility of going home was held in front of him. He would have one more brain scan to see if surgery would be required. If not, he would be able to return to his family's home in nearby Oakville.

Two nurses immediately began gluing beads to his head to map out potential surgery. Ever the optimist, Frank said he was going out to start the family van for the trip home.

When the results of the scan came back, the doctors could not explain why, but Ben had stabilized enough to return home. Surgery would not be required. They headed home, where Ben had grown up, and a two-year journey of recovery would begin.

Until Ben was drafted by the Kitchener Rangers and moved away from home at sixteen, Oakville had been home. Frank was a firefighter and Sue worked for the Town. He and his brother Chris grew up playing sports. Chris was mainly interested in soccer, but Ben was involved in a variety of sports such as soccer, lacrosse, basketball, volleyball, and swimming, in addition to hockey.

He began his hockey journey with one season of house league. From there, he played one season of AA Rep Hockey before graduating to play top-level AAA Rep hockey. In his career in minor hockey, he played in nearby Mississauga with the likes of Ryan Sproule and Remy Giftopoulos, who would go on to play in the OHL. Except for one season as a forward, Ben's entire minor hockey career was dedicated to playing defense.

Hockey quickly became the sport he excelled at. In fact, at fifteen years of age he was being scouted by several OHL teams. A potential career in pro hockey, maybe even the National Hockey League (NHL) beyond Junior, suddenly seemed to be a possibility. It would likely mean moving from home to live with a billet family at the young age of sixteen and juggling hockey with school.

Until then, Ben had never really contemplated moving from home. He was an average student at Thomas A. Blakelock Secondary School in Oakville. Scholastics were just a necessary distraction between his various sports activities. But now, his parents spoke to the various hockey scouts considering drafting Ben and suggested that they would prefer he go to a team with a good University in the community. They were particularly interested in Kitchener, London, or Guelph. There Ben would have access to a great education in addition to playing hockey. And they would be close enough to personally attend many of his games.

Ben was an elite athlete and had dedicated his life to becoming a professional hockey player. It was everything he had trained so hard for, and along with the never-ending support of his family and the Kitchener team, he would utilize that same determination to overcome this new hurdle. Head Coach Steve Spott ensured that Ben's gear and sweater remained set up in his dressing room stall and told him that it would remain there until his eventual return. It was a goal to focus on, both for Ben and his young teammates, as they worked to put the trauma of that fateful night behind them.

Coach Spott had done something important for Ben, his family, and his teammates when he told them that he would hold Ben's place on the roster open until he decided he could return. It was an element of support that reignited the competitive fire within the young man—he now had a goal to aim for. His mother might not have been so certain she wanted him to return to the game, but she put her fears aside as she supported her son's fight to overcome this injury.

It would be a long two years as Ben trained with laser-like focus. Within weeks of his release from hospital, he was back at the Auditorium in Kitchener watching his team play. Team broadcaster Mike Farwell recalls being happily surprised seeing him back at the rink so quickly. As he called the play by play for television viewers the night Ben was hurt, he thought he might have witnessed a death on the ice, so seeing the young man back in the building was reassuring.

While his return to the rink seemed fast to those around him, for Ben, it was anything but. It was one step forward and two or three steps back. The elite athletic physical conditioning and fierce competitive determination stood him in good stead. He would not let this injury stop him and he would take his recovery as far as he possibly could. He diligently applied himself to cognitive games, balance drills, walks, and a strict sleep schedule.

Two years after the accident, Ben met with neurologists. His fate was to a certain extent, in their hands—what they said would possibly determine the course of the rest of his life. They did a brain scan and when it was time to review the results, they placed that scan on one computer screen next to another that contained the scan from the night of the injury. Ben and his parents held their breaths as the surgeons told them that while they could not explain why, he had defied the odds and could return to hockey if that was what he wanted.

There is so much about the human brain that is unknown, but perhaps through sheer force of will, Ben's life was now back in his hands—from potential brain surgery to a possible return to the game he loved. It was time to meet with the team and see how far he could push himself yet again. Coach Spott had always told him the door would be open for a return, but only if he could make the team in a tryout at camp. He would have to earn it and should only come back if he was no less than 100% invested in it.

To Ben, there was no doubt. He went to camp to begin the 2011/2012 OHL season. As hockey players often say, he wanted to "leave it all out there on the ice." He would make this team (or not) through his skill and effort and nothing else. He made the team, and his goal was once again to complete his remaining OHL career and possibly play professional hockey. He played sixty-seven regular season games and another sixteen in the playoffs. The first game back was a home encounter in Kitchener. He received a standing ovation from the capacity crowd. It was totally surreal. He remembered nothing of the night of the injury. But here were thousands of people, along with his teammates and family, cheering for him. In a sense, they had all played a role in his return.

The early going of that first game was nerve wracking, but as the game went on, he felt increasingly comfortable. As the first game became more games, his comfort grew. Perhaps in a strange way, not remembering what had happened helped him in his return.

Ben went on to play two more seasons. His last, in 2013/2014 saw him proudly wear the "C" on his jersey, as he was named team captain. In his final season, their archrivals, the London Knights, asked about acquiring him in a trade. He decided to remain with Kitchener, though. The NHL New York Rangers and Nashville Predators were showing interest in possibly signing him to a minor league deal, possibly to play in the American Hockey League (AHL). Pretty heady stuff to be sure. But by late in his final year, he had decided to pivot in an entirely new direction.

Ben was already studying for a BA in Communications nearby at Wilfred Laurier University. Unlike high school, where his education was something of a distraction between his various athletic endeavours, he was becoming passionate about his studies. A desire to use the experience he acquired while overcoming his injury was burning within. He would put down roots in Waterloo and complete his studies.

His family's relief when Ben told them he was leaving his elite playing days behind, was palpable. Both for them and for him. As his final season wound down, the closer he came to the finish line, the more certain he was of his decision. There was no doubt that, while there may not have been many conscious thoughts of all he had been through, subconsciously there was a certain amount of pressure there.

While Ben had decided to move onto something new, he was uncertain what form that might take. He did not leave the game of hockey entirely; he became an assistant coach with the University of Waterloo Warriors men's hockey team.

In addition, he had begun an initiative during his final years with the Rangers. He called it "Headstrong, Fanelli 4 Brain Injury Awareness". This gave him the opportunity to speak to schools and other organizations about concussions and head injury in a positive way. After all, who had more personal knowledge of the subject than he did? And the Kitchener Rangers organization and teammates assisted every step of the way.

Ben was particularly impressed by the story of cyclist Lance Armstrong. Say what you want about the use of performance enhancing drugs (in a sport apparently dominated by them), Armstrong's recovery from cancer and return to competition was inspiring. Ben wanted to demonstrate that he, too, had made it all the way back from his injury. With the help of teammates such as Gabriel Landeskog and Ryan Murphy, he trained to compete in a triathlon. This is considered by many to be the ultimate sporting test of endurance.

In June of 2011, he participated in a 750-meter swim, a 30-kilometer bike ride and a 7.5-kilometer run in Milton, Ontario, just west of Toronto. By his own admission, Ben's body was built for hockey rather than triathlon. But, by doing this, he would support the Brain Injury Association of Canada (BIAC) by collecting pledges and selling Head Strong t-shirts for twenty dollars apiece, both at the event itself and through the Rangers team website.

Ben eventually transitioned Headstrong to the Empower Foundation. And as he continued to speak about brain injury, he was about to pivot once again. He had already achieved his BA in Communications and while he was completing that, he was becoming increasingly interested in psychology. While he might have been an average student in high school, he discovered he loved his studies at university. So, he decided to continue at the University of Waterloo by taking a master's program in Counselling Psychology.

Around the same time, he was beginning to feel that there were many people contributing so much more than he could to the study of concussions and head injury. With that in mind, he would move on to something new. He wanted to assist people by working in the behavioural and mental health space. But he had no plan on how to go about it; that is, until he spoke to a friend.

His friend pointed out that he had lots of experience speaking to people through Headstrong. It was a talent that Ben had developed at an early age; his mother had him speaking in front of people through her work with the Town of Oakville when he was growing up. He knew how to speak from the heart, whether it was for five or five thousand people.

From these early discussions came a loose plan for an initiative that became known as Heroic Minds. He would help people with issues of mental health, suicide, and disease. At the time of this writing, he has spoken to groups for three years.

He also launched a very successful weekly podcast, and the current total is more than one hundred episodes. A wide variety of guests have appeared, from those he has known personally to those he found by scrolling through the internet. He is now getting referrals from guests who have already appeared. They range from Mark Scheifele of the Winnipeg Jets, U.S. Olympic Hockey Star Amanda Kessel, comedian Gerry Dee, and fighter pilot Vincent Aiello. Each shared their personal story as Ben helped draw them out with an eye to how each story can inspire and inform listeners.

As always, since his journey began with the head injury, through Headstrong and the Empower Foundation, and now to Heroic Minds, there has been no definite plan. Anything other than a loose plan can only get in the way. In addition to the podcasts, Ben also has blogged on topics about overcoming adversity in his Heroes Journal blog.

From his own journey to overcome his injury, he has used his exposure to adversity and uncertainty to become better as a person and better at his craft. Life is not always perfect or without suffering. But these do not have to be bad. Ben feels you must get comfortable with being uncomfortable. You need to put yourself in uncomfortable situations and you must:

1. Accept your truth.

2. Know where you want to go.

3. Realize that you do not have to get there all at once. It takes patience.

You can use the pressure to grow or to be defeated. You choose how to respond. Everyone will experience failure and adversity. But from these come growth opportunities if one accepts the challenge.

Ben knows from personal experience that personal growth comes from life experience. A heroic mindset is what it takes to grow. As Ben often says, "Be the hero of your story."

Just prior to this writing, Ben decided that he will resign from his role as assistant coach of the men's hockey team at the University of Waterloo to focus full time on his studies and on Heroic Minds. Where all of this will take him, he is not certain—he does not make definite plans. But wherever he goes, he will take his Heroic Mindset with him.

CHAPTER SIX

Troy Smith

"They don't care how much you know, until you show them how much you care."

THEODORE ROOSEVELT
26th President of the United States

Troy Smith was born July 31st, 1978, in Hamilton, Ontario. He was the second of four boys born to a popular top 40 radio Disc Jockey, Dave, and Kathy, who worked for the City of Hamilton. Older brother, Christian Anderson (known to all as C. A.) was born two and a half years earlier. Next in line, Mike is two and a half years younger than Troy. The youngest, Marc, followed Troy five years later.

As one might expect, the rambunctious foursome was a handful for mom and dad. All of them played hockey at one time. Troy went on to play in the Ontario Hockey League (OHL) with the Detroit Whalers and the Plymouth Whalers from 1995 to 1999. Mike played one season with the Moncton Wildcats of the Quebec Major Junior Hockey League (QMJHL) before splitting one season between the Plymouth Whalers and the Kingston Frontenacs of the OHL. Both brothers then played Canadian University Hockey at St. Francis Xavier University in Antigonish, Nova Scotia.

Hockey played a big role in the family's life. They also billeted Major Junior hockey players from the Hamilton Steelhawks, and later, the Dukes of Hamilton. But while sports were always a big part of the family dynamic, artistic pursuits would prove a big draw as well. Father Dave was a drummer. Like his father, brother C. A. was drawn to music. And the youngest, Marc chased his artistic dreams in several ways. While he was very good at drawing things, he became known to the family as "MacGyver," after the television character who was seemingly able to make just about anything from virtually nothing. And in the middle of this was Kathy, who escaped from all this testosterone by volunteering with the Girl Guides.

Following his university career, Troy went on to play professionally. In the 2004/2005 season, he split his time between the Louisiana Ice Gators of the East Coast Hockey League (ECHL) and the Quad City Mallards of the United Hockey League (UHL). He began the 2005/2006 season with the London Racers of the English International Hockey League (EIHL) before moving on to play the remainder of the season with the Danbury Trashers of the United Hockey League (UHL).

Having taken his shot at the professional ranks, Troy then turned his attention to coaching. For seven seasons, from 2006 to 2013, he was an assistant coach with the Kitchener Rangers of the OHL. He was promoted to Head Coach with the Rangers for two seasons, from 2013 to 2015. His well-travelled career continued from 2015 to 2017 as an associate coach with his hometown Hamilton Bulldogs of the OHL. And finally, he spent one and a half seasons as an OHL head coach with the Saginaw Spirit beginning in 2017.

At the age of forty, Troy found himself unemployed. He was uncertain where his career would turn next. The answer came late in 2018. The Humboldt Broncos of the Saskatchewan Junior Hockey League had suffered an unimaginable tragedy when their team bus collided with a fully loaded semi-truck while on their way to a playoff game in April of 2018. Sixteen of the twenty-nine persons on the bus were killed. Many of the survivors suffered life-altering physical injuries and emotional trauma.

In towns like Humboldt, the townspeople are devoted followers of their junior team. They were passionate fans, and the players were celebrities. The following season, the team was struggling to resume playing while still dealing with their understandable grief. Part way into the season, changes were being made to the coaching staff. Troy was added as an assistant coach. It would prove to be a challenge unlike anything he had ever experienced in hockey. It was emotional, with signs of the tragedy found throughout the town.

Everywhere Troy went in town, he was recognized as a new member of the coaching staff. The experience was gut wrenching and yet, tremendously rewarding. Once the season ended, he decided it was time to retire from coaching.

When the season was over in Humboldt, Troy decided to move on from hockey. Growing up in Hamilton, he had friends in the Leggat family, who owned a group of automotive dealerships in Southern Ontario. He returned home to work in sales management at their Ford dealership in Burlington, close to his hometown. Using his coaching and mentoring skills, honed from years playing and coaching hockey, it did not take long for him to move into a bigger role, as General Manager of the family Acura dealership, also in Burlington.

Troy's career in hockey was in some ways, improbable. Growing up, he had to deal with kidney issues. The ureters provide a pathway from one's kidneys to the bladder. Through them, urine drips straight into the bladder and is removed from the body during urination. In his case, Troy's ureters were in the shape of a snake, with twists and turns. This resulted in the flow of urine being compromised. From age three to eighteen he was treated at the Hospital for Sick Children in Toronto (Sick Kids). At the age of twelve, he found himself in the skilled hands of Doctor Bernard Churchill. Troy underwent successful surgery to remove six inches from one ureter and eight inches from the other to allow a more normal flow of urine. When Troy turned eighteen, Dr. Churchill told the family, there were good cases and bad cases of this condition and Troy had a good one. Even today, though, he has fifty percent kidney dysfunction.

As we can see, Troy's competitive, full-contact hockey career might just as easily have been derailed before it ever began. He was allowed to play non-contact from the age of seven, and he began full contact at age twelve. But once he was able to play, he never looked back. His career in hockey led him to understand that life is a series of wins and losses. But perhaps his biggest loss did not happen on the ice.

June 27th 2007, is a day that Troy and the Smith family cannot forget. Attending the NHL Draft Meetings in Columbus Ohio, he got an unexpected phone call informing him that his youngest brother, Marc, was on life support in a Hamilton hospital and was not expected to recover. He was there because of an attempt to take his own life.

Suicide is not something one typically expects to occur in their family. Yet, according to the Centre for Addiction and Mental Health (CAMH), 800,000 people die from suicide each year around the world. Approximately 4,000 people take their own lives annually in Canada alone. And, while these facts are commonly known, it is not known how many are unsuccessful in their attempts.

In shock, Troy was on the first flight home as the family came together from various locations near and far. Dave and Kathy were, by then, divorced. Dave arrived from his home in Brantford, while Kathy made the trip from Caledonia. C. A. was living in England and Mike was in Antigonish, Nova Scotia.

Once they were all back in Hamilton, there were immediate decisions to be made. The doctors wanted to know if they would consider donating some of Marc's organs. While Troy is uncertain to this day whether his brother was an officially registered donor, it was a decision that the family quickly agreed to. Perhaps dealing with Troy's kidney issues as a child made this somewhat easier. In the end, six people benefitted from the family's decision.

Until recently, such deaths were referred to as "committing" suicide, perhaps the implication being that suicide was an illegal act. Today it is understood that such deaths are the result of mental health issues. As such, the term has been changed to "completing" suicide.

Even with new ways to refer to suicide, families and friends are still left to deal with the grief of it. Troy immediately locked down his emotions to be strong for his family. Privately, he feels that it took about five months for him to accept what had happened. Publicly sharing his emotions took several years. In the end, he reached out to a hockey acquaintance, Glenn Crichton. Glenn's daughter Rachelle had lost her life to leukemia, and in 1990, Glenn founded Coping Bereavement Groups of Ontario. This non-profit organization provides grief counselling at no-charge.

From working with "Coping," Troy was introduced to Tana Nash of the Waterloo Regional Suicide Prevention Council. Tana had personally dealt with suicide in her family. She knows that while she cannot bring back her loved ones, she can bring hope to others. Tana felt Troy had a platform as coach of the Kitchener Rangers to help others, and that it would help him as well.

Through his roles as a hockey player and coach, Troy knows that locking down your emotions is important sometimes. He recalls watching his young nephew Drew play hockey. It was late in the game and the team was down two to one. Following a play where Drew made an error that was costly to his team, he returned to the bench in tears. Ever the coach, Troy approached the bench an encouraged his nephew to be strong. The team needed a goal and needed him to keep his head in the game. It is okay to cry after the game.

The team still lost, but it was an important lesson for his nephew. To perform in life, we often need to be rational and temporarily suppress our emotions. It is okay to be open and talk about your emotions later in order to decompress.

Troy was now ready to reach out and use his public profile to speak about suicide. Tana Nash arranged for him to speak to groups in school, corporate, and government settings. He was ready to charge in with some "tough" talk. After all, if he was going to open-up to people, he might as well be direct. Not everyone would expect something other than a talk about teamwork and hockey stories. Instead, he would just hit them over the head with facts about suicide.

Surprisingly to Troy, this approach was the last thing suicide prevention groups advocate. He was counselled on appropriate words to use that might not be triggering for those in his audience who may be struggling with suicidal thoughts. He learned instead to carefully approach the subject by encouraging people to open-up and to be honest about their struggles, and to be available to those they might feel are struggling. They just need to be there for others.

As recently as five or six years ago, the medical profession was not taught how to deal with the subject. If presented with someone going through struggles, the idea was to prescribe something, if necessary, get the person calm, and release them as quickly as possible. Troy discovered this while giving a talk to medical people at a conference.

Today, he notes that there are increasing resources available to assist in this area. It is important to note that no single approach covers all circumstances. Some people respond to encouragement, such as a pat on the back. Others might be better served by straight-shooting tough talk. Also, it's important to know that not all services available to deal with mental health issues are offered free-of-charge. In Canada, one is treated for a broken arm or cancer at no monetary cost to themselves. Mental health is one area that is only recently beginning to catch up in this area. It still has a long way to go.

Troy has learned that people do not know how to act or what to say when they encounter someone who attempts or completes suicide, or their families. He knows that while it may be natural to suffer from "survivors' guilt" (What should I have done to help or prevent this?), he knows that people will only tell you as much or as little as they wish to reveal. What is important is to let these people know you are there for them. To listen, rather than to offer advice. It is okay not to have all the answers.

In Troy's experience, life, whether in hockey or the retail automotive world, is a team sport. We all have wins and losses to deal with. Hockey is only recently beginning to deal with this topic. NHL professional Wade Belak and OHL player Terry Trafford are both examples of players who completed suicide. Today, coaches and players are being given resources, so they know who and where to turn when they need help. Old ideas of "tough it out" and "play through physical and emotional pain" are slowly changing.

For family and friends who encounter those who have attempted suicide, it is important to note that old ideas of this being shameful are slowing changing. When dealing with the survivors, simply say "I am sorry," and be prepared to use the person's name who completed suicide.

Today Troy no longer speaks publicly. Instead, he concentrates on his new career managing an automotive dealership. As such, he feels he no longer has the public persona to give such talks. He thinks about Marc almost daily and believes that his young brother's death is his greatest loss in life. He also believes that life is a learning process. He subscribes to what American football coach, Nick Saban, calls "The Process." He believes in continual improvement every day.

In the quote at the beginning of this chapter, former U.S. President Theodore Roosevelt said that people won't care how much you know until you show them how much you care. Troy has seen how you can "blow people away" when you care, when you are honest, and when you end every interaction on a positive note. Things will not always go well in life. But if you establish a process of continual improvement before you encounter difficulties, chances are you can enjoy a better outcome.

Marc Smith was a bright and talented young man who seemed to have it all going for him, with a great future ahead. Brother Troy has chosen not to dwell on the loss, but rather to know it is okay to deal with your own mental health struggles. He knows that we all have different coping mechanisms. He grinds his teeth at night, so he wears a mouth guard. He exercises to burn off stress. And he loves going to movies alone so that he is not distracted by anyone. Through Troy and others like him who have suffered such a loss, we can all learn to be more self-aware when dealing with our own struggles, and to be more open to the struggles of others.

Troy does not know when or if he will return to speaking publicly about suicide. But he will always be better prepared to reach out to others who may be struggling. He lives now to show people how much he cares.

CHAPTER SEVEN
Danielle Campo-McLeod

"In my struggles is where I found my success."

DANIELLE CAMPO-MCLEOD

Thirty-six years ago, Steve and Colleen Campo were busy parents of two very active young boys. Kenny was six and Craig was five, and both were becoming active in sports such as hockey and baseball. Into this mix entered the girl they had always hoped for. They had no idea of the adventure that lay ahead for them and the newly arrived Danielle.

The family lived in Windsor Ontario, immediately across the Detroit River from Detroit, Michigan. The whole family enjoys sports, and they were fans of the Toronto Maple Leafs and Major League Baseball's Detroit Tigers. They went on walks as a family, and it was when Danielle was about two years of age that they noticed some developmental differences from what they had experienced with their boys.

Rather than using her full foot, she walked on her toes. She would walk a few steps and fall. She would reach for her parents to be picked up. If she did pick herself up, she used a wall or a tree to pull herself to her feet.

Colleen was a social worker who specialized in child behaviour and was very familiar with children's development. Perhaps she thought that Danielle, being a girl, was on a different development trajectory than that of her brothers. As time went on, she even wondered if her daughter had flat feet and required orthotics. Danielle finds this amusing today because she admits to having "ridiculously high arches."

When Danielle was two years old, Colleen decided to have her checked out by a specialist who would perhaps prescribe orthotics. It seemed like a simple enough appointment, so she took Danielle to see the doctor while Steve was at work; he was employed at the General Motors Trim Plant. What happened next was life changing for Danielle and the entire family.

After watching Danielle walk down the hall, the doctor shocked Colleen with an immediate diagnosis of Muscular Dystrophy (MD). According to the Muscular Dystrophy Canadas web site, MD:

"is a term used to describe a group of more than 160 different neuromuscular disorders characterized by progressive deterioration of muscle strength. The causes, symptoms, age of onset, severity and progression vary depending on the exact diagnosis and the individual."

The diagnosis was later confirmed when they visited a specialist in London, Ontario for a second opinion.

Even today, with decades of research into MD, it is still somewhat misunderstood. It is believed to have a hereditary component. Yet, there was no apparent family history. Experts suggested that the occurrence of MD in Danielle was perhaps a one in seventy-five billion chance.

The family was stunned by the diagnosis. Colleen's initial reaction was one of anger whenever her daughter fell. But eventually, they would turn to their faith as they learned to celebrate successes and deal with failure. Dealing with the extreme highs and lows soon became a part of life with their daughter.

When Colleen and Steve first got the news, their first thoughts were that they did not know a lot about MD. They thought of comedian Jerry Lewis and his annual Labour Day Telethon for MD, and their minds went to the worst-case scenario for their daughter. Danielle was prescribed physiotherapy.

As one might imagine, asking a two-year-old to do the required exercises proved challenging. It was suggested that they change the therapy from dry land to water-based to make it more fun for Danielle. The young Danielle loved it, but her parents hated the water.

Soon, another challenge presented itself. In order to correct her strange gait when she walked, doctors performed hip surgery at age four. Danielle's muscles were not holding the left hip in its socket, so they built a barrier to ensure the hip remained in place.

Danielle was placed in a body cast for four weeks. Parents everywhere are likely sympathetic to the trials and tribulations of keeping an active four-year-old entertained with her body encased in a cast. But, ever determined, she was up and walking despite the cast within three weeks. There was no holding her back.

Meanwhile, attempts to identify the specific type of MD continued. Initially it was thought that she might have a severe form known as Spinal Muscular Atrophy. Later the diagnosis would change to Congenital Fiber Disproportion. Over the years, there were numerous painful muscle biopsies and other tests, continuing to the present-day, as doctors remained puzzled by Danielle's condition.

As her water-based treatments continued, it became apparent that Danielle loved being in the pool and had a talent for swimming. In fact, a coach asked Colleen and Steve if they knew about the Paralympics. They did not but were open to their daughter participating in the Program.

As a young child, Danielle began competing locally in Windsor. As she grew, it became apparent that she had considerable ability in the pool and soon was competing seriously. She preferred the sprint events such as the fifty and one hundred, but her coach encouraged her to compete in the four hundred endurance event as well.

By competing in the longer event, Danielle began to improve her sprint times. The pain of competing in the four hundred, in effect, made the sprints feel shorter and less strenuous. Her mental approach in all her events was thus improved.

While swimming was her main interest, there was a brief flirtation with hockey. As previously mentioned, the entire family was sports-minded. If you wanted to hold your own during the family dinner table conversations, being a sports fan was a must. From a very early age, Danielle attended her brothers' hockey and baseball games. When hockey was finally offered to girls in an integrated league with boys, she decided to give it a try. As one might imagine, skating while dealing with MD would prove challenging. Her stick got a real workout as it was used liberally to assist her in remaining upright. Danielle was pleased when she managed to score her first goal in her first game. The only issue was it came on her own team's net, bringing her budding hockey career to an end as quickly as it had begun.

At the age of twelve, Danielle underwent another major surgery. This time, it was on her feet. As previously mentioned, she had difficulty walking flat-footed. The issue, as it turned out, was that her heel cords were too tight. The doctors decided to lengthen them surgically. Typically, this surgery would be performed on each foot individually, with a delay between them. But being as active as she was, Danielle had both feet operated on at the same time.

The surgery was painful; the ligaments, when lengthened, try to return to their original state. The result was painful muscle spasms. She was placed in non-walking casts for six weeks and the plan was then to be placed into walking casts. But, just as when she had the hip surgery at age four, Danielle would not be confined. Just three weeks into her recovery, she shocked her parents and the doctors by walking in the non-walking casts.

At last, Danielle had better balance and more endurance. She could more easily get down into the starting blocks when racing. She was also, by then, in a school that had disabled, and fully abled kids integrated into the same classrooms. It was the early days of such integration and everyone, teachers and students included, was learning how to deal with this new world.

One of her teachers was somewhat puzzled when it came to Danielle. Some days, she would present herself to the class as pretty much able-bodied. But on other days, she could present as somewhat lazy and uninterested, holding her head up with her hands. The teacher had heard of Danielle's competitive swimming and decided to visit a practice to see for himself how determined and strong she could be. After seeing her in the pool, he better understood that, while she was limited in some respects regarding her everyday life, she had virtually no limits in the pool.

Life for Danielle was becoming normal in most respects. There was some bullying from the other kids in school, but she took it in stride. She preferred to focus on her time in the pool. There, she would not be held back. And it was there that she was becoming increasingly competitive in her drive to reach the Paralympics.

By the time she was fifteen, Daniel held the world record in each of the fifty, one-hundred, and four-hundred freestyle events. And it was these performances that would carry her to her first significant experience on the world stage when she qualified to attend the Paralympics in Sydney, Australia.

The Paralympics run parallel to the Olympics and are held every four years, immediately following the Olympics. They generally use the Olympic venues and consist of mostly similar sports. In Danielle's case, she was a freestyle swimmer competing in the fifty meter, one-hundred meter, four-hundred meter, and the four by one-hundred relay.

Accommodations are made to account for individuals' specific disabilities and strengths. There are ten classifications ranked from one (most severe) to ten (least severe). Danielle raced in the four events within her classification. As anyone who follows Olympic events knows, they can be very political when it comes to making subjective decisions related to issues such as classification.

It was the year 2000, and Danielle's memories of stepping off the plane upon arrival are still vivid. Swimming is possibly the most popular sport in Australia and Australians are perennially among the best in the world. It seemed like everyone knew who she was as they welcomed her into their shared passionate love of swimming.

What really stood out for young Danielle were the huge venues and the large crowds. One hundred and ten thousand people attended the opening ceremonies. One might expect someone as young as fifteen might feel considerable pressure under such circumstances. But perhaps her naivety favoured her—she could not understand what the fuss was all about. After all, weren't they all simply trying to touch the wall first, just like in any other race?

Perhaps the pressure caught up to her in her first race, though. As the world record holder, she was the obvious favourite in the four hundred going in, but she finished second by two one-hundreds of a second. A photo of Danielle, crying in the pool at the conclusion of the race, was seen in newspapers across Canada, accompanied by headlines talking about the pain of losing. Instead,

Danielle explains today that people did not understand that she was simply overwhelmed by the experience of competing in the large venues in front of the huge crowd.

She would redeem herself by winning Gold in the fifty and one hundred metre races. The entire experience was surreal for the teenaged Danielle. It would, however, leave her with memories to last a lifetime.

After the Summer Olympics in Seoul South Korea in 1988, Canadians became very familiar with the protocols of testing for performance enhancing drugs, thanks to the story of sprinter Ben Johnson. The experience at the Paralympics is no different. Because of the diverse nature of the physical conditions experienced by Paralympians there are drugs in use that are not seen at Olympic Games. However, these must be pre-approved by the Paralympic Officials and cannot be muscle enhancing.

For elite athletes such as Danielle, drug testing before and after competition is a straightforward fact of life. It is interesting to note that Danielle was not on any medication when she competed. There quite simply were no known drugs that might be of benefit for her condition at that time. So, in lieu of drugs, she used swimming as her medication.

Before returning to Paralympic competition in Athens, Greece four years later, there were significant changes in Danielle's life. She enrolled at McMaster University in Hamilton, Ontario. This meant leaving her family home near Windsor. She had decided to enrol in pre-med and would also train there. In her first week, though, she saw how heavy the textbooks were and quickly changed her major to Psychology.

Her time in Hamilton was limited to only one semester. Her coach moved to Calgary, Alberta and Danielle moved even further from home so that she could continue training with him. Rather than enrolling in university in Calgary, she chose to focus solely on swimming.

After the 2004 Games in Athens were complete, Danielle decided to retire from Paralympic Competition. She returned to Windsor and attended the University of Windsor, where she studied Social Work. She was also working for Muscular Dystrophy Canada.

More changes were forthcoming over the years. In 2012, while on vacation in Florida with friends, she met an IT professional named Denny McLeod. When they both returned home to Windsor, she and Denny went on their first official date. They went to Joe Louis Arena in Detroit to see an English Rock Band known as "Muse." Anyone who has been to Joe Louis Arena will remember its seating as very steep, a challenge for most able-bodied people, and even more so for someone afflicted with MD. Danielle was concerned with having to explain her limitations while on her first date.

She need not have been concerned. It seems that prior to the date, Denny had injured his knee playing football with friends, and was hobbled himself. With both of them being physically limited, it made Danielle feel more comfortable than she might have normally been.

Apparently, the date was a success, and the two went on to be married. Not only did she now have a husband in her life, but also two young children from Denny's previous marriage. Calum and Ella now also entered Danielle's world of Muscular Dystrophy. The kids adapted quickly, and they learned that when they played tag, Danielle was always it. But in the pool, she could never be caught.

Ella, being very young, was apparently impressed by Danielle, and even took to mimicking her way of walking. At first Denny and Danielle were somewhat concerned that something might be wrong. Eventually, they figured out that Ella was simply copying her new hero, and they managed to convince her to return to walking normally.

Callum on the other hand, adapted relatively quickly. When he noticed she struggled sometimes with curbs, he instinctively held out his hand to assist. If you ask him and his sister what it is like to live with someone living with MD, they shrug it off by saying the only real issue is having to stop playing video games to help carry the laundry basket up and down the stairs.

Callum and Ella are now teenagers. They have been joined by Corbin, who is now four, and Samson, now two. She recently gave birth to another child, a girl named Morgan. They reached the decision to have children together, after careful consultation with medical experts, who did not have a lot of definitive information for them. The doctors did suggest, though, that there was not necessarily an increased risk of inheriting Muscular Dystrophy. To this point, all are healthy and active. Danielle is simply their mother.

Now in her mid-thirties, Danielle has spent most of her life living with her diagnosis. She was therefore unprepared for a phone call from her McMaster University neurologist, Dr. Mark Tarnopolsky in 2020. She was waiting in line to have a blood test when her cell phone rang. He shocked her with news that he believed she was not afflicted with MD at all.

She knew that Dr. Tarnopolsky continued to be relentless in his pursuit of finding out more about her condition. He was always testing gene after gene and in the process, he had discovered an unnamed gene that was causing the nerves not to communicate properly with her muscles. This was huge news, after years believing that the muscles were malfunctioning.

Dr. Tarnopolsky had expected that Danielle would eventually weaken to the point where she would be confined to a wheelchair. Instead, she seemed to be stronger than ever. While he was a big believer in using sports to get stronger, he was not certain why she was not weakening as one might normally expect for someone dealing with MD. He suggested that by taking two relatively common drugs, they might be able to speed up the messages from the nerves to the muscles. They were Epinephrine and Mestinon.

As one might expect, Danielle needed some time to process the suggestion that after decades of believing she had MD, she might now have a new prognosis. She immediately left the line for the blood test and returned home. Dr. Tarnopolsky forwarded the prescriptions. Danielle immediately filled them and took the medications, not knowing what to expect. Within an hour, she began to see improvement.

Today, Danielle notes that she can climb stairs more easily. She can perform squats more readily when working out. She holds a pen more comfortably. She does not tire as easily, and her body no longer hurts all the time. She was somewhat confused by the latter—she had almost never experienced not being in some type of pain. She checked with Denny; he confirmed that it was not normal for someone to be in constant pain.

Dr. Tarnopolsky evidently was not expecting such a fast change. He could not believe what Danielle was telling him, and he had her visit him in

Hamilton so he could see for himself. Like her, he is learning more about this development as time goes by. In fact, he was about to have her stop taking some of the medication to see how she would respond. But news of her pregnancy immediately changed the game plan, and she was taken off all the medication. Much to the surprise of all, Danielle still appeared to be gaining strength. The experience of expecting a child for the third time is different from the first two.

After completing the Paralympic Games in Sydney in 2000, Colleen got the fifteen-year-old Danielle involved with public speaking as a way of giving her pain a purpose. Now, twenty years later, she still does motivational speaking. She turned to this easily and loves connecting with people. She never writes out a speech ahead of time, preferring to speak from the heart. She looks out into her audience and is happy to see the "light go on in people" as she speaks. In short, she gets back as much or more than she gives during these talks.

Danielle continues to work for Muscular Dystrophy Canada as a Director, Client Services. She was about to begin attending the University of Windsor to take her Master of Social Work. But that plan was put on hold while she is awaiting the birth of the new baby. In addition, she may one day write a book about her experiences. Safe to say, as stated at the start of her story, Danielle has used her struggles and become infinitely successful.

CHAPTER EIGHT
Margot Page

"Life is too short."

WILLEM VERLAAN

"Control what you can control."

MARGOT PAGE

Scarborough Township in 1964 was in the middle of a huge development boom. The Toronto suburb was growing exponentially. Into this, Margot Verlaan was born. She was the third child of Willem and Marijke Verlaan. Sister Monique, four years older, and brother Marcel, two years older had preceded her.

Willem, known as Wim to his wife, and Marijke (Marique to her friends) had immigrated to Canada from the Netherlands following World War Two. Willem was a bank manager, a job that entailed moving frequently as his career progressed. Better known to his friends as "Bill," the joke was that name roughly translated to "butt" in Dutch. Still, he never allowed that to hold him back.

Willem grew up near Amsterdam and, as a teenager, he worked peeling potatoes for the Nazi occupation forces. He would bring the nutrient-rich peels home each day for his family to eat.

Marijke grew up near Rotterdam. Her parents had split when they were young. She lived with her father, a doctor. He provided refuge in his home for Jews looking to hide from the Nazis. Marijke's mother and sister lived elsewhere in the Netherlands.

The War had a dramatic effect on both Margot's parents. Like many of his generation, Willem internalized the experience, rarely speaking of it. Marijke, on the other hand, grew to truly appreciate everything she has.

Willem was a soccer fan, while Marijke was not interested in sports. The kids, however, loved sports and rarely missed opportunities to participate. Monique was competitive in cross-country and distance running and Marcel played hockey and baseball. Younger sister Margot was perhaps the most athletically gifted one in the family.

As a youngster, Margot would follow older brother Marcel into hockey arenas along with the family to watch him play. She soaked it up, coming to love the game and wanting to play. At one point in her father's career, the family was living in the Northern Ontario town of New Liskeard. Marcel took Margot out onto the frozen lakes, where she would play goal while he took shots. But she wanted even more and would eventually take off with the puck while he chased her. Her love of the game was permanently etched into her psyche. Little did any of them know that the game would become her life's calling.

Soon, Margot was pestering mom and dad about playing organized hockey like Marcel. At the time, girls' hockey was not common. Today, girls are sometimes able to play with the boys, especially at younger ages, but her parents did not realize that could even be an option for their daughter. So, being unable to locate a girls' team in New Liskeard, they got her involved in gymnastics and track and field instead.

While Margot would prove proficient in these sports, they were poor substitutes for hockey. Life, however, works in mysterious ways. Soon, Willem's career would see him on the move once again, to the town of Kincardine, on the shores of Lake Huron. Margot was tired of constantly moving and was reluctant to uproot her life once again. Dad, however, had an ace up his sleeve. There was a girls' hockey team in Tiverton, about a ten-minute drive from their new home. Suddenly, Margot was interested.

After the move, Margot played for the Tiverton Big Reds. Some of her team-mates were twenty years older than she was, but she would not be deterred from playing the game she loved and was soon excelling.

It was not long before the family was on the move again. This time, their new home was about ninety minutes south, in Kitchener, Ontario. She joined the Plattsville Raiders, a Women's Senior C team, and her hockey educa-tion continued. But once again, life would take a turn. Willem and Marijke separated, and eventually divorced. Willem moved to Ridgetown, in South-Western Ontario, where he later remarried. Marijke remained in Kitchener.

Margot finished high school in Kitchener and moved to Hamilton to attend McMaster University (Mac), where she played for the Women's Varsity Hockey team. While there, she also played for the Burlington Wolverines, and she competed in both shot put and discus for Mac. She had also com-peted in these events in high school. In her senior year at Mac, she was named Female Athlete of the Year.

Margot went on to Western University in London, where she earned her teaching credentials. She was accepted into the "Physical Education, Math, Science Teacher Education Program" (PEMSTEP). This is a specialized program, and entry required an application, good grades, and a formal face-to-face interview. Students taught for one-half year in one school, and then returned to Western to attend in-class academic commitments and courses in order to graduate.

Margot began her teaching career at Courtland Senior Public School in Kitchener. As always, she threw herself into her teaching, both in the class-room and in the gym, with all the enthusiasm she could muster. At the same time, she continued her hockey career with the Burlington Wolverines of the Central Ontario Women's Hockey League. When they were eliminated from the playoffs, she was picked up by the Hamilton Golden Hawks. Later she would play for the Toronto Aeros.

While Margot was extremely talented as a player, there was always the nagging disappointment that unlike in men's hockey, there was no well-defined path to follow to pro hockey or international hockey following university. People sometimes asked why she did not choose sports such as volleyball or basketball where there was more opportunity to compete beyond school, but she remained undeterred and continued to play hockey at the highest available level.

Her patience would eventually be rewarded. By the late 1980s, Women's Hockey was on a path to hold its first World Championship. The first event would be played in 1990 in Ottawa. Margot was thrilled by the prospect and wanted to be a part of Team Canada. To get there, she would have to go through a series of tryouts against the best the country had to offer. Unlike the men's event, where players were invited by Hockey Canada to attend the tryouts, with all costs covered by Hockey Canada, Margot and all fellow competitors would have to pay their own way.

Margot was all in and would spare no personal expense to be in Ottawa at the inaugural event. There was a regional tryout, then a provincial, and finally, a national team camp. She made it to the national camp, ahead of eventual Hockey Hall of Fame players Angela James and Geraldine Heaney, who also made it to the camp, but would be added to the team later.

World Championship tournaments for the men were held annually. The women, at that time, played every two years. Success followed quickly for the women, with Canada emerging victorious in 1990, 1992, and 1994. While with Team Canada in 1994, Margot mentored fifteen-year-old Hayley Wickenheiser. Margot's veteran status and teaching qualifications meant that Hayley would get help with both her studies and her hockey development on her path to the Hockey Hall of Fame (HHOF) in Toronto. During her HHOF acceptance speech, Hayley paid tribute to the role Margot played in her early years with the national team.

By 1998, Margot came to one of life's forks in the road. She was good at teaching but was tired of working within a defined curriculum. She wanted to push the boundaries in her career and define her own successes and failures. An opportunity presented itself—an interview with Niagara University, outside Buffalo, to be Head Coach of the Women's NCAA Division One Hockey Program. She was intrigued and drove with her mother to the University to explore it further. Marijke went along to shop at the area's famous discount outlet malls while Margot attended the interview.

When the interview was over, Margot picked up her mother and as they were returning home to Canada, mom asked how it went. She was shocked to learn that her daughter had accepted the job on the spot, despite having to work in another country for less money and security than her teaching career offered in Canada. Given her longevity and success, the transition from player to coach seemed a natural step.

At the 1998 Olympic Games in Nagano Japan and the 2002 Games in Salt Lake City USA, she was able to expand her experience in the Game by working with the Canadian Broadcasting Corporation (CBC) as a television colour commentator for the Women's Hockey coverage. This is a role that she also performed at several World Championships. Along the way, she worked alongside some of the best hockey broadcasters in Canada, such as Gord Miller and Paul Romanuk. Ultimately, she decided that broadcasting was not for her. Other quality female hockey commentators such as Cheryl Pounder and Cassie Campbell-Pascal have since followed in her footsteps.

Margot continued at Niagara until 2010. Along the way, she took a sabbatical in 2006 to be an assistant coach with Canada's Olympic Team. This role reunited her with Hayley Wickenheiser, this time as a coach. In this role, Margot came to truly appreciate how driven Hayley was to succeed. In one example, Hayley asked to meet with her, and announced she had some set plays for faceoffs. Margot had been working with the team on such plays in her role as Assistant Coach. If any player other than the veteran star had requested such a meeting and asked for such input, it might have been thought unusual, to say the least. For Hayley, it was just another example of her drive for excellence and her expectation that others would work as hard as she did.

Margot has experienced coaching both as a head coach and an assistant coach. As an assistant, she was something of a buffer between the players and Team Canada Head Coach Mel Davidson. Women, perhaps more than men, want to know why they are being asked to perform in certain ways. It is more than just systems to them. As her career progressed, Margot has come to realize that she cannot be too rigid with her players, and it's necessary to allow them to be creative on the ice as well as in life.

When her contract was not renewed at Niagara in 2010, Margot had to find new ways to support herself. She did some mentoring and coaching at Oakville Ontario's Appleby College, west of Toronto. Appleby is a private high school-level college, and this move had her working once again with younger, teenage athletes.

From Appleby, she worked with the Swiss Women's national team in a mentoring role. Women's hockey has, until recently, been dominated by Canada and the USA. If the game is to continue to grow, teams elsewhere must develop stronger programs. Margot has seen this happen. Since her time in Switzerland, the Program has hired a female General Manager, and Sweden had an all-female staff guiding their athletes at the World Under-18 Championship when it was held in St. Catharines in 2016. The result has been improved performances at World Championship and Olympic competitions. The women's game now seems to be in good hands.

Since 2017, Margot has found stability and security as Head Coach of the Brock University Women's team in St. Catharines, Ontario. Prior to this, she helped the Women's Hockey Program at Brock for several years before being given the Head Coaching Position. At time of writing, the world has been in the throes of the Covid-19 pandemic. Play has been suspended for more than a year, and an entire season went by with players getting very little ice time as they tried to stay sharp for a hoped-for return to play.

Covid-19 meant no games, few opportunities for practice and training, and was difficult for the athletes. For several of her players, their university careers are ending on this unceremonious note. While the women's game now provides more opportunities after school ends, it still has fewer options than those available to its male counterparts. The National Women's Hockey League (NWHL) provides some opportunities, but it still does not offer a living wage. The Professional Women's Hockey Players Association (PWHPA) does offer chances to participate in special events and tournaments. But these do not provide a regular schedule or season. There are also some chances to continue playing in Europe, but not as many as for the men.

For Margot, all this has proven frustrating. Progress for the women has been painfully slow for her, but she acknowledges that there has been considerable progress since she took up the game. It is difficult sometimes when comparing opportunities for women versus the men. Nowhere, perhaps, is this more evident than when her alma mater at Mac came calling, looking for financial support. When she asked if any of the funds would be used for women's sport, the answer was no. It would be used to assist the men's football team. Angrily, Margot suggested they call her back when they were raising funds for sports such as women's hockey.

Margot has thirty-plus years of coaching experience and over forty years in the game when you add her playing days. She has thrived on working under pressure. When she could have had security as a teacher, she followed her heart into playing and coaching the game that she loved. As evidenced by her immediate acceptance of the coaching job at Niagara University, she has always been driven to succeed. As Willem told her growing up, "Life is too short." Margot has taken this to heart. She has constantly reinvented herself by living for the experiences life offers. To live life, one must make bold decisions.

This is the philosophy she advocates for her athletes as well, and extends off the ice, too. Recently, one of her athletes, who starred in both hockey and rugby at Brock, was offered the chance to try out for Canada's Olympic bobsleigh team. Uncertain whether to accept the opportunity because she had never participated in the sport, Margot convinced her to go to the tryout. Even if she did not make the team, she would have a wealth of new experiences to draw upon in life. Not only did she attend the camp, but she also made the team, and Margot can take pride in encouraging her to try something new.

A stubborn drive to succeed seems to be something Margot was born with. Her mother recalls that around two years of age, she disappeared one day. Marijke found her inside a nearby fenced-in playground. Mom scolded the other kids playing there for letting someone so young unescorted into the playground. They protested that they did not let her in, but rather that she had scaled an eight-foot-high fence. Uncertain whether to believe them at first, the kids convinced her to take Margot outside the fence and see what she did. Marijke hid behind a tree and could not believe her eyes as she watched her youngster climb up and over the fence to rejoin the kids on the other side.

Margot has always been someone open to new experiences and following her heart. She would rather try something and possibly fail at it than to regret not trying. This attitude is one she has cultivated in her young athletes as well. But the longer she has been coaching, the more patient she is with them; she has realized they do not have the same life experience as she does. She has become increasingly aware of also teaching life skills and assisting with mental health challenges. Brock has made increasing numbers of mental health resources available to all its students.

Margot has learned that, as much as life demands pushing her to succeed, she must also allow herself some downtime for the sake of her own mental and emotional well-being. She now practices mindfulness techniques and meditation. She lives on a small farm on the Niagara Peninsula. She loves animals and being alone in the barn with her horses, cats, and ducks. She works out regularly and for the past seventeen years has followed a strict vegan diet.

In addition, Margot has returned to her earliest hockey roots. When the opportunity presents itself, she works as an instructor at hockey camps for youngsters just learning the game for the first time. In this non-competitive environment, she can enjoy watching the kids learn that the game is fun. From this vantage point, Margot enjoys the fact that young women now have hockey heroes to look up to just like the boys do. There are now at least limited opportunities to play pro hockey in addition to the national team programs. The sport is growing worldwide. Women are now being admitted to the Hockey Hall of Fame. And opportunities to coach are increasing all the time.

Margot has never taken the "safe" or "secure" path as she has lived her life. As seen in her quote at the beginning of this chapter, she "controls what she can control" as she has carved out a career in hockey. When hockey was not available to her as a youngster, she took up gymnastics, shot put, and discus. Eventually she would incorporate training techniques learned in those sports into her hockey experience.

In short, Margot believes that we must push ourselves past our comfort zones by going "all-in" when living life. This leads to continually reinventing ourselves as we lead our lives. This is a lesson we all could learn. After all, as Willem said, "Life is too short."

CHAPTER NINE
Cyril Bollers

"Today I will do what others won't, so tomorrow I can do what others can't."

JERRY RICE

Former National Football League Player

If people are doubting how far you can go, go so far that you can't hear them anymore."

MICHELE RUIZ

Entrepreneur, Broadcast Journalist and Public Speaker

I n 1971, a young single mother from Georgetown, Guyana was looking to provide a better life for her young son. Doreen would leave family behind as she preceded her son to Canada, where she would work to establish herself while sending support back home. Four-year-old Cyril Bollers would follow his mother to his new home two years later. Neither knew what the road ahead would lead them to.

Mother and son lived in the Oakwood suburb of Toronto prior to moving to Scarborough. Cyril was athletically gifted and gravitated towards most sports, including hockey. Soon he was following the National Hockey League's Toronto Maple Leafs. Rocky Saganiuk was his favourite player and more than anything else, he wanted to wear his hero's jersey. Cyril also wanted to play hockey, like many of the kids he was growing up with. At more than three hundred dollars, competitive rep hockey was out of the question as Doreen concentrated on providing for their "needs" rather than their "wants." Less expensive house league hockey would have to suffice.

Life in Canada was very different for Doreen and her son. Perhaps foremost among the differences was that they were persons of colour now living in a predominantly white society. They would never allow this to hold them back as they adjusted to their new lives.

Doreen married and Cyril suddenly had an alcoholic stepfather who could be abusive. The relationship also produced two brothers, Wilmot, and Dwayne. While the family had its issues, it also brought discipline. Cyril had to ensure he was home each day to be certain the dishes were washed, and the house was neat and tidy. No matter how late he was out on Friday nights, Cyril was up by eight o'clock on Saturday mornings to perform chores such as cutting the grass. While his relationship with his stepfather had its issues, by the time he passed away, he had made amends.

For Cyril, his mother would always be his biggest supporter. Values derived from her deep religious faith showed her how to teach perseverance, determination, and responsibility. As we will see, her efforts still guide him in his life's pursuits to this day.

As mentioned earlier, Cyril loved sports. While he did not get to play a lot of ice hockey, he was able to play at a high level in the less expensive ball hockey. He also played first base and left field in softball and fast ball. In high school, he took every opportunity to get out of class by participating in as many sports as possible.

Growing up, money for luxuries was not readily available. So, when young Cyril was looking to get a new baseball glove, he felt fortunate to convince his mother to splurge on one. At first, they looked at one for thirty dollars. But one for seventy dollars had caught Cyril's eye, and Doreen decided to spend the extra money. They took the glove to the cashier who rang in the sale. But before paying for it, Doreen felt something was missing—a glove for the other hand. For seventy dollars, she felt there had better be two gloves. She was surprised to learn that in baseball, you play with only one glove.

Finally convinced, she made the purchase and Cyril proudly took it home. Unfortunately for him it would be stolen a few weeks later.

He also was a two-way player on the Woburn Collegiate high school football team where he was a defensive end and tackle. His coach was former National Football League and Canadian Football League player, Jon Henderson.

Cyril left high school without graduating to work for Steven and Michael Wise at the Wise Group of Companies. The brothers hired the eighteen-year-old to run a night club and several restaurants. He gained a wealth of real-world business experience in return for pay and a rent-free apartment. They made him feel like family, and he thought, why would he go to school when he had several credit cards in his wallet and could afford most things he would ever need or want?

Eventually, though, he returned to complete his high school diploma. He went to work in Social Services with "At Risk Youth" involved in the Correctional System, first at Kennedy House Youth Services, where the clients were teenage boys aged twelve to eighteen. He was there for four years, and he learned to deal with teenagers who were out to test the limits, knowing he could not physically restrain them. Discipline learned from living and dealing with his abusive stepfather was put to the test.

He was then moved to Manse Road, a facility dealing with teenage women involved with the Correctional System. He put in twelve-hour days, teaching the women they would be held responsible for their actions. He learned to be positive in outlook, and he came to grips with the fact that he would not always be able to help them. In many instances, he taught them that not all black men were pimps or drug dealers. In return, he learned to be the best version of himself.

Like his young charges, Cyril sometimes found himself confronted by police because of the colour of his skin. On one occasion while working at a restaurant, he pulled into the parking lot. He parked at the far end of the lot beside what he thought was a friend's car. When he discovered the other vehicle did not belong to his friend he decided to move to another spot. As he began to move the car, he found himself confronted by police who were vigorously questioning why he was there. Only when an employee of the restaurant intervened and explained that Cyril worked there did they release him. He did not immediately react to this situation, but two days later he found himself in tears as he thought about what might have happened.

Another time, he was waiting for a train at Scarborough's Kennedy Station. Police were in pursuit of a suspect who happened to be black when they came across Cyril standing on the platform. His mother, who was working for the Ministry of the Attorney-General, had taught him to do the opposite of what the police typically expected from a young black man. He remained outwardly calm, always kept his hands in plain view and made no sudden moves. Again, he was eventually released without further incident.

These incidents have given Cyril real world experience of what life can be like when you are black. Along with recent world events, such as the death of George Floyd in Minnesota at the hands of white police officers and the rise of the Black Lives Matter Movement, have shown him how easy it is to be in the wrong place at the wrong time. They give him pause when he talks about this with young people today. They help him show his humanity and help him relate to the young people he works with.

When Cyril was in high school, he met Michelle Guy, whom he eventually married. At the time of writing, they have been married for twenty-five years, and they have three children. Cassandra is twenty-eight and grew up playing soccer. Cyril Junior, or "CJ" as he is known, is twenty-five. He was drafted by the Ontario Hockey League's (OHL) Guelph Storm and played briefly in the Ontario Junior Hockey League (OJHL). The youngest, Kyle, played in the OHL for parts of three seasons, and for parts of two seasons in the OJHL.

Hockey was a big part of life for the family. CJ played house league hockey in his youngest days. Cyril watched his son's games and witnessed the coach of the team giving his own son preferential treatment and extra ice time. When Cyril asked if he could assist with the coaching, he was politely turned down. The inference he took from this was, "What do you know about hockey? You are black."

Not one to be deterred by this rejection, Cyril found a way to get into coaching at the house league level. Eventually, he was asked to take over the more competitive Select Program. Normally the team played a thirty-game season.

But Cyril was all in, and he worked to involve the kids in as many games and tournaments as possible. They ended up playing eighty games, and he worked to learn as much as possible about coaching. For him, knowledge gave the program power and as his knowledge grew, so did his coaching involvement; he also coached at the Rep Level for teams such as the 1995 birth year Toronto Red Wings.

He tried to coach one year ahead of CJ. So, when CJ was playing for the 1996 birth year Red Wings, he was coaching the 1995 birth year team. This allowed Cyril to get as much coaching experience as possible, while not being so critical of CJ's development. He learned the hard way, from CJ, that he needed to be supportive of his son instead. After watching his son play a game one day, Cyril was being critical of something that happened on the ice. CJ apparently had enough, and he told his father not to come to his games anymore. This was a tough life lesson for Cyril, but he has worked to hold the kids he works with accountable both on and off the ice while at the same time showing them respect.

The more he coached, the more Cyril wanted to coach. He was always striving to grow and develop. He took every Hockey Canada Course he could, and along the way, he obtained his Hockey Canada High Performance One and High Performance Two Certifications. At the same time, he continued to coach at the highest competitive level he could. He believed in inclusivity and giving all players an opportunity to play the game. But he also recognized that not everyone had the resources to play. Thus, for over twenty years now, he has developed and operated programs to give kids of colour an opportunity to play when they might not otherwise be able to afford it.

Cyril became involved with Skillz Hockey, a program of hockey development for kids of colour. Then, together with Wayne Ho-Sang, he formed the Black Aces spring and summer program for high performance athletes. This is an inclusive program for all kids. Initially this began as a one-week hockey skills program for ninety-nine dollars. Initially there was a surprisingly poor response and turn-out. But when it was later changed to a spring/summer program, it took off and became popular.

In the meantime, coaching rep level hockey teams continued, and included kids of all colours. National Hockey League players such as Darnell Nurse,

Josh Ho-Sang, Justin Bailey, Mark Friedman, Brendan Lemieux, and Carter Verhaeghe all played for him. Colour was never an issue in the dressing room. But racism was encountered on the ice. One particularly humorous time came in the room between periods of a game. Brendan Lemieux, who happens to be white, gave a speech about how the other side was not showing them any respect because they were black. Everyone in the room immediately realized what was happening and were soon laughing about it.

That incident showed how everyone who played for Cyril put team ahead of all else. His teams would always enter and leave the rink together. This was partly for their own protection and partly to psych out the other side. "Us versus Them" is a common theme on his teams. One of his teams won an impressive thirty-two tournaments, with only three losses. Two came in the semi-finals and one in the final. The NHL uses the brand, "Hockey is for everyone." But for Cyril and his young players hockey was for everyone long before this.

Cyril has studied the game and has also become well-read while looking for ways to motivate his players. This reading has included books such as *The Art of War*. Out of this has come a reputation for making powerfully motivating speeches. He comes up with these the night before a big game when he has trouble sleeping. If they happen to be playing in the United States, he might use "America versus Canada" to motivate his players. In local tournaments, he might use the "Sacrifice" theme. Respect for your opponents and your teammates are big parts of his motivation as well.

Passion is a big part of everything Cyril Bollers does in life. He believes in himself and is always looking for opportunities to grow as a coach. For ten years he worked for Maple Leafs Sport and Entertainment (MLSE) at what was then known as Ricoh Coliseum (now Coca Cola Coliseum). This is the company that owns the NHL's Toronto Maple Leafs, and the Coliseum was also home to their Toronto Marlies American Hockey League (AHL) Affiliate Team.

Officially, Cyril was the Suites and Catering Manager. While there, he took advantage of the chance to reach out to people like Brian Burke, who was at that time Vice-President of the Leafs. He also talked to Kyle Dubas who then was the General Manager of the Marlies, and coaches Sheldon Keefe and

Steve Spott. He promoted his accomplishments in the game and asked how he could get opportunities to interview for coaching roles with the Leafs East Coast Hockey League (ECHL) Affiliate team. He was rewarded by being given the opportunity to practice the injured Marlies while the team was away on one road trip.

While no further coaching roles were offered at MLSE, Cyril continues to reach out today to his contacts in the ECHL and AHL. He does not use the "black card" and does not ask specifically to be hired. He instead asks for the opportunity to interview and have them get to know him as a hockey coach. He also makes sure he stays in contact with Hockey Canada to ensure he remains in good standing. If he does make it to the professional ranks, he wants it to be a result of his hockey qualifications. People such as confidante Jason Payne, who had a pro hockey playing career from 1996 to 2005 and is now an ECHL head coach, have shown him it is possible to be black and have a career at the highest levels of the game.

While professional hockey has yet to reach out to him, Cyril is always looking for new opportunities in the Game. One such opportunity is his involvement with the Jamaican Olympic Ice Hockey Federation (JOIHF), first as an assistant coach to their first head coach, Graham Townsend. This was a chance to get in on the ground floor, while at the same time providing new black players with playing opportunities.

Graham Townsend recognized that Cyril had access to players of Jamaican descent through the Black Aces in Toronto. Cyril was able to provide twenty of the thirty players in the program. When Graham left to run a USA-based hockey school, Cyril was promoted to head coach, a role he has held for four years at the time of writing.

The team has won tournaments such as the Amerigol Latam Cup, and the JOIHF are now partially sanctioned by the International Ice Hockey Federation (IIHF). Until now, the team has relied heavily upon Jamaican players living and playing in other countries, particularly Canada. The goal is to ultimately develop native Jamaican players. The next step will be to provide a fully sanctioned IIHF program. For that to happen, they need a rink to be built in Jamaica to provide grass roots development programs. Plans are now being formulated by the Jamaican government to build a rink with both Olympic and NHL-size ice pads. Training facilities and a hotel would be attached. In a Caribbean country that put a bobsleigh team into the Olympics, it would seem anything is possible.

Meanwhile, back in Canada Cyril continues to advocate for young black players. He is hoping to make his Black Aces Program non-profit. The game is still very expensive and often beyond the reach of young black players. He is looking for corporate sponsors in his quest to make the game more accessible to all. For him, it is about more than hockey.

Cyril is always looking to promote black talent in the game of hockey and the game of life. In March of 2021, the California-based AHL Ontario Reign put an all-black forward line on the ice—Quinton Byfield, Akil Thomas, and Devante Smith-Pelly. This is widely believed to be the first professional all-black line since the 1940s, when a line known as the "Black Aces" played together. The 1940s line included Herb Carnegie, Ozzie Carnegie, and Manny McIntyre. Later in the 2021 season, the NHL's Tampa Lightning iced an all-black forward line consisting of Evander Kane, Dustin Byfuglien, and Johnny Oduya.

When these events happened, there was considerable media coverage. While Cyril believes that being given the chance is good for the game, he wishes that they would simply be lauded for being "first" to accomplish this, that they simply could be players looking to develop their hockey careers rather than being "black."

Off the ice, young black players are now looking to grow the black experience in the game as well. Akil Thomas and Elijah Roberts were Major Junior teammates together with the Ontario Hockey League's Niagara Ice Dogs. Akil is now playing pro hockey in the AHL, and Elijah has begun a University Hockey career with Ryerson University in Toronto. Together the two have been hosting a widely listened to podcast known as "Soul on Ice," which is supported by the National Hockey League. Elijah is a graduate of Cyril's Black Aces Program. Cyril hopes he was a small part of these off-ice developments. Some might call him mentor to young men such as these. But he feels this makes him sound old. He prefers instead to be thought of as a "friend" or "colleague."

Cyril's reputation continues to grow. He recently watched with great interest when players he worked with won a World Under-18 Championship for Canada. These were Wyatt Johnston, Ethan Del Mastro, and Danny Zhilkin. He coached them on the 2003 birth year Marlboros. He has also been interviewed on Rogers Sportsnet's "Hometown Hockey" by Tara Sloan, and on CTV's "Your Morning" by Ben Mulroney.

Cyril Bollers is now widely regarded as a talented and successful hockey coach who just happens to be a person of colour. He continues to learn every day that life is about much more than hockey. It is about teaching life skills, building relationships, and managing personalities. It also includes being transparent, speaking from the heart, and building trust. He inspires youth by speaking to schools about his "real life" stories of struggles and triumphs.

He sees the NHL now working to provide increased diversity. It is a process that will only be deemed a success once he sees Black, Indigenous, People of Colour (BIPOC), and women in management roles. He does not believe that others can hold him back, and he continues to promote himself at every opportunity in his continuing quest to build his career. As an example, Cyril is now a member of the Board of Directors for the Greater Toronto Hockey League (GTHL).

Now in his early fifties, he is a grandfather to Alaia. He wants his own children and those he coaches to have more chances for success than he had. Family always comes first. He looks to control what he can in life and to surround himself with positive people. If others stand on his shoulders, he will consider himself to be a success.

CHAPTER TEN
Final Thoughts

"Success is not final; failure is not fatal: it is the courage to continue that counts."

WINSTON CHURCHILL
British Prime Minister During World War Two

The preceding stories demonstrate the resilience of the human spirit. Sometimes we all wonder if we can forge ahead with life. The people profiled here are no different than you and me. They have all been faced with challenges that can seem insurmountable. Yet they have all successfully confronted their challenges and led fulfilling lives as they continue to succeed in pursuing their hopes and dreams.

We can be forgiven sometimes if we look at others with a hint of jealousy as we wonder how they got so "lucky" in life. Why can't we be so "lucky"? But it seems that, when you drill beneath appearances, you discover that there are no overnight successes. Nobody escapes failure. No one escapes being confronted by challenges. And yet, more often than not, we try to hide our failures and challenges, or to blame others.

By sitting down and writing about our lives, if we are truly honest with ourselves, we can look back and discover that, in addition to failures, we have had successes too. Failure indeed was not fatal. Our challenges and failures make us uncomfortable and rightfully so. Without such discomfort, we might never demonstrate the ambition to grow or to truly appreciate success in life. To quote Ben Fanelli in Chapter Five, "we all must learn to become comfortable with being uncomfortable." This concept was written about in more detail in a book published in 2011. Entitled "Get Comfortable Being Uncomfortable" and was written by Bob Molle, He won Silver while representing Canada in Wrestling at the 1984 Olympics in Los Angeles. then went on to win two Grey Cups as part of the Winnipeg Blue Bombers of the Canadian Football League.

It seems there are no overnight successes. As I discovered when I decided to start this book by sharing my story, there is nothing unusual about being a "late-bloomer." A lot goes into building a life story. And if that was true for me, I felt it must be so for others as well.

I was not disappointed. I will be eternally grateful to all these individuals for being so honest and open in sharing their stories. My broadcasting buddy Ed Burkholder lost both his parents at a young age and overcame cancer on top of it. Jim Thomson was prepared to overcome a dysfunctional upbringing to achieve his dream of playing in the NHL, only to have to face his alcohol and drug demons. Mike Farwell honours the deaths of two sisters to Cystic Fibrosis every day, while en route to living his broadcasting and fundraising dreams. Ben Fanelli demonstrated that he could alter his childhood professional hockey dream by using his catastrophic brain injury as motivation to help others. Troy Smith recognizes his emotions every day following the suicide of his brother. Danielle Campo-McLeod believed for most of her life that she had Muscular Dystrophy, only to discover, after setting Paralympic swimming records, that she does not have MD. Margot Page overcame the odds to forge a career and life as a woman in hockey. And Cyril Bollers has worked all his life to overcome racial stereotypes to create a life coaching hockey, and along the way he is bringing diversity to the game.

Failures. Successes. Lives well lived. And they are not done yet. Not by a long shot. These are lessons we can all learn as we lead our lives. If only we can take the opposition and adversity and be grateful for the good things we have in our lives. Sometimes they are small, but I honestly believe the good things are there if only we are prepared to look for them.

If I could leave you with one final thought, consider the words of Stephen Covey, the author of the best-selling book, *The Seven Habits of Highly Effective People*.

"I am not a product of my circumstances. I am a product of my decisions."

This is certainly true in my own life, and I believe it to be true for those individuals written about here. May you all make wise decisions.

ACKNOWLEDGMENTS

Like many sitting at home during the long days of the Covid 19 Pandemic, I looked to find a project I could work on that might prove meaningful. Sitting down and writing a book would have hardly seemed possible to me prior to this time. But having thought about it, I decided to plunge in, despite never having written anything significant since my university essays.

This project began with my own story of undiagnosed Tourette's Syndrome and the effect this had on my life. I was not and am not looking for sympathy but rather hopefully greater understanding. For my parents, Jack, and Helen, it was a story of never giving up on finding answers for their questions and mine. It took decades but eventually answers and treatment were found. They both have been gone for some time now, but I would like to think they would be proud of me for chronicling not only my story but the others in this book as well.

For my brother Bob, despite being seven years older, you had a rink side seat in this journey as well. You have never been anything less than supportive. I could never have accomplished this book and other successes in my life without your example to guide me.

My wife of over thirty years, Doreen and our son, Jason have been my rock upon which I have been able to build my life in recent decades. Your steadfast belief in me has led me to accomplishments that I might not otherwise been able to achieve. For Jason especially, your artistic and musical creativity have shown me that I too might have something creative to offer in the form of this book.

If not for a long-time friend of over forty years, I might not be where I am today. Bruce Craigie led me to become a Big Brother, which in turn brought both Doreen and Jason into my life. In addition, he provided me with the opportunity to grow professionally in the automotive industry when he introduced me to the world of Honda Canada. Your friendship and belief in me when others did not, always provided encouragement.

Chris Cuthbert is someone I have known since our days in high school together. A mutual love of sports and broadcasting is what probably led to us be friends during that time. The fact that you would take time out of your hectic professional and personal schedules to write the Foreword for this book is something I will always be grateful for.

Since my final year of university, I have been pursuing my broadcasting career in one form or another. I met Carl Hiltz and Steve Bashak at McMaster's CFMU-FM and we have been friends ever since. When I needed to know during the early days of writing this book if I was on the right track, I knew I could count on them to read the manuscript and provide honest feed-back. Thank-you.

Of course, it goes without saying that when you set out to write about the lives of others and their impact in the world, it would be virtually impossible without their cooperation. For your patience, kindness, and willing-ness to share through countless Zoom Calls, Phone Calls and Email Exchanges, thank-you.

In addition to the subjects of this book, bringing their stories to print would not be possible without a publisher. Debbie Anderson, Carly Cumpstone, and the entire team at FriesenPress have proven infinitely patient and wise in guiding this rookie author to the finish line. To them, I will always be eternally grateful.

Finally, there have been many persons without whom, I would not have achieved whatever modest success that I have to this point. People like Producers Brad Scott and Darren Sawyer and hundreds of others in front of and behind the cameras. Others too in the Automotive Industry as well. Friends from school and university days. There is no way I can mention you all without missing someone. Please accept my thanks for making my life richer for knowing you all.